Playing Sideways

*Golf Stories, Escaping the Rough of Life,
and Playing England's Best*

ERIK C. HANSEN

PLAYING SIDEWAYS

Golf Stories, Escaping the Rough of Life, and Playing England's Best

ISBN: 979-8-9885147-5-6

Book Layout by Transcendent Publishing

Printed in the United States of America.

"Cinderella Story…outta nowhere…"

– Carl Spackler (Bill Murray)

CONTENTS

Introduction: Acknowledgment of a Pro............................ ix

Switching Gears, Right Out the Front Door........................ 1

In a Time of Need…a Friend 7

A Little History 9

Tales and Fails from the Rough 15

A Lot to Think About…Again…In Mere Seconds. 27

Strategery... 31

Looping in Caddies (pun intended) 35

Teeing Up for Later... 43

Out of Our Comfort Zone, We Go................................ 49

Fake It…'Til You Can Make It 57

The Moment of (a) Character................................... 75

My Home of Golf 81

The Rota Shed-jule (that's Brit for Schedule)................... 97

The Yanks Arrive, One by One 99

Royal Cinque Ports - Course 1, Day 1 103

Royal St. George's - Course 2, Day 2.......................... 113

Princes - Course 3, Day 3 125

"Lechyd da!"... 135

Royal Porthcawl - Course 4, Day 4 143

Pen-Y-Fan, Brecons Beacons - Day 5 (The Supposed "Day Off") 149

Royal Lytham & St. Annes - Course 5, Day 6 177

Formby - Course 6, Day 7 193

Royal Birkdale - Course 7, Day 8 203

Royal Liverpool - Course 8, Day 9 215

The Final Transfer - Day 10 233

Match Play 237

The 19th Hole (Epilogue) 245

In Closing 253

Course Rankings by My Overall Experience 255

About the Author 261

Dedication

To the best four women of my life: my mother, my sister, my wife, and my daughter. Past or present, their perspective, guidance, support, approval, and love have continued to let me do things like this and fill my soul.

To all my friends who endured my many questions about this book. In its many forms and rewrites, there was never a doubt that it was my first attempt, but you all supported and helped without judgment. I pride myself in having the best friends and you all proved as much throughout the process.

Finally, to my father. An unwavering example of how to be one. I enjoy doing things like this just to see your reaction. Thank you for guiding me through life and teaching me all that you have.

Introduction

Acknowledgment of a Pro

Last year I played some of the most famous and challenging golf courses in all of Southern England…with six people I'd never met. This trip fell into my lap at a time when I could least likely afford it but most definitely needed it. In this book, I hope to take you, the reader, along with me as we share the courses, towns, and pubs we enjoyed for nine fantastic days and nights. But first, let me describe how I came to this decision to leave my busy work and family life for more than a week and spend a bunch of money on that once-in-a-lifetime golf trip. You see, this book…well… started with another book.

One of my more powerful influences of this past year is a man who truly inspired me to take a new journey in life. His name is Tom Coyne. Tom is the author of several books based on playing golf on hundreds of courses in both Europe and America. From trying to keep up with the pros on tour to literally walking from course to course throughout all of Ireland (yes, he logged over eleven hundred miles on foot with a backpack and his clubs), his storytelling is amazing. But the book that really got to me was his journey of playing one hundred and seven courses in Scotland in fifty-seven days to qualify for the Open Championship. *A Course Called Scotland* hit me squarely between the eyes and stirred my being at a time when I least expected it.

With my mom ailing from dementia and accelerated Alzheimer's and my dad struggling to keep up with this rapidly declining situation, I suggested to Dad that we both read this book and share stories when on the phone. My hope was that the conversation would distract us from the dire updates and bad situations over which we had little control, and it worked; it made things better.

Tom's storytelling would take me and Dad back to Scotland: a place and a time, ten years past, when we had visited and played the most worshiped of golfing destinations – St. Andrews. Tom kept us turning the page with tales of playing "our" courses; Turnberry, Carnoustie, Kingsbarnes, the New Course (founded in 1895), and of course, the granddaddy of them all, The Old Course. Story by story, he took us along from town to town, course to course, and pub to pub, all while sweeping us out-of-body and into an ethereal plane of page-turning companionship, founded on the greatest game on earth.

Not long after I accepted this invitation to play some of England's finest golf courses, I reached out to Tom, mostly to say thank you for helping my father and me through a difficult time. At the end of the note, I shared the details of the trip and asked for some advice; How does one prepare for (spoiler alert!) nine rounds in ten days?"

He replied graciously with (and I'll spare you the emotional parts about my situation):

"Sounds like a fantastic itinerary – enjoy every minute. Eat that full breakfast – you'll need it. And bring some band-aids for the blisters. And lots of Advil. And stay hydrated! Robert was useless by day four!"

Note: You'll need to read *A Course Called Scotland* to learn about Tom's life-of-the-party friend Robert who accompanied him in Scotland to play golf… only to never make it to a single tee box.

Overall, these books encouraged me to embrace this trip of a lifetime and, not only participate but put keystrokes to electronic paper with feverous alacrity and take others along for the ride. I hope you enjoy it.

Switching Gears, Right Out the Front Door

The mind is an incredible machine, and it's amazing to me how fast it can process things in a situation of self-inflicted crisis.

On Dec 14, 2021, against the history of so many injuries, the scary stories of so many before me, and the wishes of all my golfing buddies, there I was, halfway down a section of trail appropriately called the "Boneyard," mid-air and fully dismounted from my pricey, over-engineered electric mountain bike thinking at least a hundred thoughts in the half-second it took to come back to Mother Earth. Here are the few that I recall:

Damn it…Not again!! Okay…just don't land on your head…Come on…tuck and roll…and Get out of this walking…Wife's not gonna be happy…airlift to hospital…

but somehow, strangely…

Golf.

It just popped in there.

Playfully, mountain bikers have a colorful vocabulary for the sport and thus a handful of fun nicknames for crashing. OTB, is an abbreviation for "Over the Bars" ("Out the Front Door" might also paint the picture), that moment when the bike stops moving for any variety of reasons while your person continues forward up and over the handlebars until you meet your painful destiny lying somewhere out in front of you. Imagine someone being thrown out the front door of the bar and into the street and you're pretty much there.

Another sad, yet hilarious example is the resulting "Yard Sale" that happens when the body hits so hard that all associated rider gear is jettisoned in multiple directions, thus looking like your neighbor's scattering of random, one-dollar items across the lawn three Saturdays a year.

The fact that these colloquialisms exist and that their definitions can be extrapolated from their names may be reason enough for most people to never throw their leg over a mountain bike. I remember reading a survey that was taken by an outdoor magazine, whereby mountain biking was named the most dangerous sport out there. I can attest to this statement because, in my experience, there's a very fine line between glorious, dirt-enabled fun and a broken collarbone.

After many years of riding bikes and experiencing these terms first-hand, I have little defense for those questioning my reasons for continuing to do so. To most of my sane friends, I'm sure mountain biking at my age sounds like mid-life crisis nonsense, but the fact is that riding has always been my mental therapy. Unless I crashed, I always came home happier than when I left. A ride in the morning with The Dirtbags (my mountain biking group) would put life into balance and perspective and help me deal with anything that came at me during work or throughout the day. My wife Nicki could attest.

Though we aren't steady churchgoers now, I grew up with a God based upon my confirmed Lutheran learnings. However, I had seemingly found another version of a deity, just minutes from my driveway in Laguna Canyon Wilderness: where nature, companionship, and adrenaline met to form a two-wheeled elixir for baptism.

As a result, whenever I was in a bad mood Nicki would let me know and send me out of the house to speak with that God of the Mountain and tell Him all my problems so I would come back healed. And it worked – well, usually. I'm not sure what I did to deserve it, but on this day I would find out yet again that the God of the Mountain can be vengeful as well, and It was about to show me how much.

Where were we? Oh right...still headed "Out the Front Door." As gravity brought me back to a dry, packed *terra firma*, the backside of my helmet hit first; and, as I continued my attempted tuck and roll, I landed on a rock with the back of the neck and shoulder blade.

Ow.

In a moment of terror, I felt a hit to my spinal cord just off center, awakening a sense of vulnerability.

Please not there.

Ironically, in my attempt to "take it easy," I was bringing up the rear of my morning group. As I went through this crash landing, I let out a loud, curse-word-of-a-scream to let the guy before me know I was going down, and going down hard. It worked. He heard me and turned around and hiked back up the trail just in time to see me post-crash, in full yard-sale mode, standing up a dusty mess while swearing at myself yelling, "That's it!!! I'm done with this s#*t!!"

As I slowly came to my feet, I felt lucky that no bones seemed broken and all my extremities were working; but at that moment, a sharp pain like a knife pierced my left forearm two or three times and then my hand went numb. Nerve damage.

Golf thoughts again.

Riding like this at my age and with my injury history seemed flat-out reckless and yeah, I should probably have quit years ago. The funny thing, though: I used to think the word was spelled "wreckless," but it now occurred to me that what I was doing at fifty years young was wrecking more, not less, so that just doesn't make sense. Having separated both shoulders, sustained multiple concussions, broken my wrist, bruised ribs, and endured various other sprains, it didn't make sense at all. But I've continued to do it, loved almost every minute of it, and survived most of it.

But others hadn't.

A month before my crash, a local man (my age with a family) and another young man (a professional motorcycle racer) had both died riding the same trails I rode regularly (may they rest in peace); so there's that. I had also crashed halfway across the park no more than eight months ago, and hit my head, injuring my neck. So, what better thing to do coming off a neck injury (which had sidelined my regular life, sleep regimen, and golf game for months), than tempt fate yet again…and lose. I guess I'm just a slow learner. Real slow.

So close to the holidays, this crash was a perfectly terrible ending to the most difficult year of my life.

Four months earlier, we had lost my mother, who had been in rapid decline from Alzheimer's - this, in addition to my sister's passing from breast cancer two years earlier. Mom was put in a home because Dad could no longer handle it on his own; however, the home itself became a major problem. Mom had taken a horrible fall while left unattended, which resulted in our pulling her out after one short week. Relocating her required an exhausting effort by my father and it had nearly killed him. Thinking he had finally shored up a good hospice space and that she was stable, he joined me on a short vacation to take a break from it all. Only two days in, we got the call that she had passed in her sleep. We were devastated. After this, I nearly lost him to the resulting stress and, even worse, a broken heart.

Despite the support of my amazing in-laws, who had helped throughout my mom's medical issues, I felt like I was on my own. The mental trauma was unfolding and thrown upon me like a dark blanket, and I had no tools with which to cut my way out. I always knew the time would come to take care of my parents, but it seems you're never really prepared. And, with my mom and sister gone, I now had the sole responsibility of ensuring my fathers' health. Mom and Dad had been the best of parents growing up, so I owed them both at least that much. However, this meant splitting my time between my own family in California and Dad in Arizona, helping him as much as I could, knowing it might never be enough. It was a tough realization and pulled at me every day.

Contributing to my depression – I had been sidelined from most things athletic due to the surgery I'd had on a torn ligament in my right arm six months earlier. I was a bit of a mess both mentally and physically, to say the least.

Yet as I struggled to get dressed and even brush my teeth, I kept thinking about golf. Maybe it was because I knew my mountain biking days were numbered and golf would be all that was left. Or, maybe it was because if I didn't recover I might lose golf – the one sport my father and I played together for most of my life. Overall, I knew after multiple back surgeries in my thirties I had been here before and any attempt to get back to playing normally would result in the game getting ugly. And it did.

In a Time of Need...
a Friend

"It's always darkest before dawn." This has been quoted so many times that it's probably lost some meaning, but back in August of 2021, in the mid-darkness after Mom had passed, my friend Alan reached out with a phone call – a phone call that would mean a lot.

Alan and I met while working together in tech almost twenty years ago, and, put simply, he is one of my favorite people. He had transferred from Kansas within the company back to his native home of Southern California and his work ethic was a marvel to me. He was the best salesman I'd ever met, period. A cold-calling machine of unprecedented relentlessness, yet so cordial and so effective. When he left the company and moved out of tech to sell insurance, it was no surprise that he built his business faster than the normal agent and continued to do great. I was thankful for the short time we worked together, and we stayed friends - talking about golf and courses we played (and wanted to play), which made the workday go faster. In fact, our wives became great friends, and we ended up even taking our kids to the same daycare! This made for fun times at dinners and parties, and it had all stemmed from our shared love of the game.

As a result of all these commonalities, we played a lot of golf over the past twenty years, and as many times as we'd played, I was always amazed at how good of a mood he was in; how he chatted up the others, complimenting them, joking *with* them rather than *at* them. And he was philanthropic – still is. At his young age, he currently sits on the board of Folds of Honor – a charity that raises money to provide scholarships for children of fallen military personnel. He's simply the type of guy that makes others better by being around him, so, yeah, when Alan calls, I pick up.

During the call, he told me he had been doing golf trips with his buddies (mostly from the University of Kansas, where they played golf together) for years now. Knowing everything I was going through, he was keen to mention, "Hey, we're headed to the UK to play next year and if there's an opening, I'll slide you in… 'cause you'll love these guys!" He went on; "This trip is nine rounds in ten days with eight guys! Oh, and six of the courses are British Open Rotation venues in England." That was a lot of numbers and I'm just so-so with math, but that sounded pretty good.

"Thanks for thinking of me, buddy," I replied, "I'll keep it in mind!"

He knew I needed something like this…he could sense it in my voice. In fact, Alan had no idea how much I would need this in months to come.

So, you're telling me there's a chance…

A Little History

I've been lucky enough to play this game of golf for most of my life. It's been my dad's only real sport, and he introduced me to the game when I was very young by taking me along on rounds with his friends. Before I had my first real set of clubs, he had me hit with this little club he called a "Cleek " (or "Chipper" here in the US). It looked a lot like a putter but was a bit of a cheater club for people who could not chip well. They would just use a putting stroke and let the loft of the club lift the ball onto the green to get it rolling.

As goofy as this little club was, it was all mine and it's responsible for my favorite memory in golf. When I was about seven, Dad and I were at the local Antioch municipal links having a game with his buddies. We came up to the 11th hole, which was a nice little downhill par 3, at maybe a hundred yards. While we were still rolling up to the tee box, I anxiously hopped out of the cart, ran over, and teed it up while he chatted with his friends. I can still remember how tacky the black leather grip was on this little cleek, and, without a single practice swing, I just hit it.

The ball left the tee with purpose and made its way airborne down to the green and landed about thirty feet from the hole. I rushed back to my dad, tugged on his shirt, and he said something like, "Yeah, go ahead and hit when you're ready." What? We had missed the whole thing! Now, I can't remember if I said anything as I didn't talk much back then (which my friends would never believe now), but I know I pointed in the green's general direction while still holding a fistful of his shirt. I remember at least that much, for sure. He went up to the tee box and looked down to confirm it.

He was as shocked as I was and told his friends, "Guys, come take a look!" They all commended me once they peeked over the edge of the tee and down to the hole.

"Nice job, Erik!" said one guy.

"Now you need to make the putt!" said another.

Yeah right! I'm seven... one miracle a day, buddy!

After everyone hit their shots, we loaded up in the carts and drove down to the green, all the while my dad giving me a proud slap of approval on the knee (which he still gives me to this day). When my time came to putt, Dad handed me his putter.

"Now finish it up." he said, "Go on."

I approached my ball timidly and lined it up as best I could. With little regard for speed and direction, I just hit it. It wiggled with maybe three bounces left and two to the right (Antioch was no Augusta!) on its way to the hole and went in! I could not believe it. No one could! All his friends went nuts. I remember being so shy and embarrassed that I immediately ran over and hid behind Dad, using him as a shield from any direct eye contact. They all calmed down (in order to approach me like the small forest animal that I was) and came over and shook my hand like gentlemen in a gentleman's game. My first birdie.

From there I was hooked, playing and practicing with him whenever I could. Hitting putts in the living room, asking when we could go to the range, et cetera. Excited at the thought of a prodigy, my dad bought me a starter set by Northwestern that had a "bag" made of a vinyl plastic tube with my name painted on it (at a three-dollar surcharge). In doing some research while writing this, I found these clubs on eBay for sale listed as a "Vintage Northwestern Pro-Bilt Starter set." Poppycock. I'm only fifty-one and nothing I've ever received as new can be vintage just yet, if for no other reason than I'm just not ready to be that old. On the other hand, I just used the word "poppycock," so maybe eBay seller "watchsports2011" is right. Vintage, indeed.

Still, these clubs were pretty sweet for a tyke like me, and I used the hell out of them. My dad also subscribed to *Golf Digest*, so each month I would tear through it reading all the instruction tips but mostly pouring over the swing photos of a young Jack Nicklaus and Tom Watson whenever they were featured. I practiced the short game indoors and nicked my share of coffee tables at home and, while showing off, almost killed my friend's grandma.

Yeah, you heard that right. I almost killed little Billy Martin's grandma while practicing my swing – oddly enough, during a garage sale. She walked right behind me, and I got her right in the forehead on my backswing. Tough old gal, though - she managed to stay on her feet and everything. I had never felt so bad in my eight-year-old life. Sorry, Grandma!

The young game of golf was bliss, and I was picking it up as quickly as I could. My dad couldn't have been happier. But, as I got older, testosterone would come into play. This, coupled with the fact that I was Norwegian meant my attitude could and sometimes would overcome me without understanding. It just happened. Alas, with my Viking temper, this game would cause such fire-breathing, mentally twisting anguish that would result in those clubs being thrown during, or going in the trash after, a bad round. Embarrassingly, a few outings ended in a bent or snapped shaft after a snap hook, sending my mind and my ball off the reservation. It brought out the true me, as it does in most golfers, and I didn't like what I was seeing. So, that was it. Around the age of twelve, I decided golf and I needed to go on a break and "see other people." Tennis anyone?

Looking back, there's no doubt I made the wrong choice there. Had I been able to control my temper, I probably could have been a decent high school player and even gone to college for it. But, being a rebellious teenager, I was still doing everything I could to avoid becoming my father. To give you some perspective, this was a man who was a successful salesperson and played golf with customers at places like Pebble Beach and the Olympic Club. For free! Kids are dumb and this was proof I was still a kid. So, I played tennis and got good enough to start teaching at fourteen, playing in high school, and, eventually, coaching. I even thought of making a career out of it. At one point I was a twenty-three-year-old assistant coach at Long Beach State, recruiting and training Division 1 athletes. It was an amazing experience, but that was pretty much the peak for competitive tennis. I continued to teach kids on the side during and after college to make money, but I lost my love for playing it when my knees and back started acting up. Eventually, I would give up tennis and start mountain biking, which sounded like a good idea. Little did I know...see above.

As for golf, I could never truly walk away from that mistress of the links. While in college, I played for fun – mostly with my friends as we snuck onto the local municipal courses in Long Beach with a twelve-pack of beer playing 'til the sun had nothing left to offer. In fact, we got so good at that process, I wrote a paper on it for my P.E. golf class. I have no doubt that, with one eyebrow up and the other one down, the professor both loved and admonished, "The Effects of Drinking on Golfing." Thanks for the A, Dr. Husack.

Over the past thirty years, the game of golf has given me so much in terms of friendships and continued playing time with Dad, creating memories and conversation fodder to last a lifetime. I knew I could never completely walk away and was glad as hell that I didn't. The duality and metaphorical ties between the game and life are ones that simply cannot be denied.

While I was writing this book, a good friend shared an interesting point of view regarding life and golf and it had to do with playing from the rough. He followed up on this by saying,

"…not just playing out of it or escaping it, but somehow enjoying the process and the challenges it can present, and then learning from them." This really resonated with me.

We built upon our conversation with the fact that, in essence, life is rough. We never aim to be there, but when living our lives or playing the game we find ourselves there quite often. And, remarkably, a few of us lose sight of the fact that although we're there, we're still playing and still have options – it's only temporary. Not even the best lifers or golfers are in the fairway all the time, but, when in the rough, they know how to recover quickly and play it safe when needed, making sure that they are still in the game. The key to getting through it – and out of it – is experience and knowing when to be conservative, play it out sideways, and give yourself a better shot.

Sadly, many golfers consider the act of playing sideways as one of surrender followed by a walk of shame. For sure, it is tough to accept that you've landed yourself in this situation due to a bad shot or a bad break in golf or life respectively – and that you might have to bail yourself out with a conservative play. After all, there is no full lash at the ball. No glory. No highlight reel. But most fail to realize that the gutsy play you were considering – that impossible full swing from the thick rough, or around the trees, or over the water, or all of the above, and onto the green – seldom finds glory and only leads to more trouble.

So yes, we agreed that there's a lesson to be taken by the best in golf: realize when you need to take those lumps and play out sideways with your head held high, because, after all, it's a thinking head with plans of minimizing that bigger mistake.

Tales and Fails
from the Rough

For the record, attempts had been made to escape from the proverbial rough that year. I felt like the grass was as deep and finding my purpose on this beautiful blue marble called Earth was as hard as it had ever been. The problem was, I just kept hacking away, forcing the issue, and going for the metaphorical green instead of just playing smart and sideways.

The first such effort came while on vacation in Mexico, before the bike crash and about two months after Mom's passing. The wife and I both needed to get away from work and home life and so, one Sunday, after a few margaritas and Mexican food with our best friends, we hopped on our laptops and scheduled a quick weekend with them south of the border. It was one of those all-inclusive packages at an affordable (but nice) resort. Once the itinerary was confirmed, it wasn't long before I decided I would sneak in an early-morning round of golf to avoid the heat and play while Nicki was sleeping off a possible hangover from the night before. All things had gone according to plan as we neared our departure, so I decided to check the forecast and ruin my day. Yup, there it was…one day of rain; and of course, it locked onto the one day I could play. I figured it couldn't be that bad, right? It's Cabo…! Desert!!…Cactus!!! How much could it rain? Click. Tee time scheduled.

The weather had been pretty good our first day there, so I had some high hopes as we turned in that evening. When I woke up at five a.m. and hopped on the hotel shuttle it was still dark out, but as the miles and minutes passed, I noticed the skies remained pitch black. Small openings of light popped through the clouds, giving hints of time passing, but after checking in at the pro shop and heading to the range to hit balls, it wasn't getting any better. As I continued to warm up, I strained my eyes to see my ball go off in the distance, but then I spied something more ominous: lightning strikes just off the coast. Frequent pops of white illuminated the skies like flashbulbs, showing me details of the accumulating cloud formations and the gloomy fate I was in for.

Maybe it will blow over?

We teed off in low visibility, and as the light gradually presented more landscape over holes 1 and 2, it seemed there was a faint chance my playing partners and I would remain dry. Leaving the number 2 green, we crossed under a highway with anticipation as just beyond it was the most picturesque hole on the course: the ocean hole 3rd. I hit my tee shot in a waste area that bordered the fairway down the entire right side of the hole, so I played out sideways and then overhit my second shot well past the green. The ball would come to rest next to a cabana lounge on the largest bunker on the course – the beach! After a casual drop, I managed to play out sideways (yes, again) onto the green and buried a long putt for an exhausting bogey. This "double sideways" attempt followed by the long putt had to be an omen, because within minutes the heavens opened up and hit us with a downpour so bad the highway overpass behind us quickly turned into a waterfall, blocking off the main route back to the clubhouse!

Our retreat turned out to be nothing less than a reckoning. What started out as a lovely seaside golf course had turned into a water park. As a result of this manifested detour, our trip back was three times longer and would end up stranding my playing partners when their cart conked out after attempting to cross a wash-turned-river-rapid experience. We had to use one cart to push out the other and barely avoided getting both stuck. As we limped into the clubhouse looking like drowned rats, my mood lightened when I came upon a good friend Dave Tetov (who I had also run into at the airport upon arrival), dry as a bone and waiting out the storm. We got caught up and I was relieved to hear that they were here celebrating his wife Kristin (who is a professional horse rider-shower) and her win over Hodgkin's lymphoma. This news brightened my morning, but, sadly, did nothing to dry my clothes. Deciding not to wait out the storm, I returned to the hotel soaked and a little pissed for the rest of the day. To cap it off, upon exiting the return shuttle I was greeted with, "Oh, senior, you tried to play golf in this??? We only get weather like this about four times a year!"

I had timed it perfectly. How awesome.

I failed to get out of my mental bunker that day and it ruined a perfectly good vacation. In hindsight, I realize that to even be thinking so negatively meant I was still not ready to return to contentment. I was forcing it and decided to gamble regardless of the signs telling me to cancel the round. Lesson learned?

Not a chance! Two months later, in January, post-bike crash and following weeks of physical therapy, I felt that with enough Advil and stretching, I could tee it up (again, I don't know when to quit) and schedule a small weekend golf trip to the California Desert for my birthday. Desert golf with Dad and two friends Cliff Ward and Scot Grimes (aka "Cliffy" and "Grimey") seemed like a good idea but slowly turned into a disaster that was both scary and hilarious. This time the weather was amazing, but it became a weekend of wrong tee times, wrong courses, poor play (from the neck injury), and finally a hair-raising crescendo on the final night before our last round. A night we'll never forget.

We had rented a house in a decent neighborhood on the border of Indio and Palm Desert. After a fun night of dinner and drinks, we laughed ourselves silly watching Jimmy Fallon and Will Ferrell perform their "Tight Pants" skit from *The Tonight Show* - a classic. My dad was not as well-versed in this newer form of late-night comedy, so he turned in around ten. I followed suit around eleven with an announcement about as nonchalant as I could make it: "Well, I'm heading to bed since we have an early tee time tomorrow." Cliffy and Grimey didn't take the bait and refilled their drinks. Oh well. No worries.

As midnight came, those two knuckleheads were somehow getting louder as they carried on a heated debate around the overall records of the 49ers and Rams; and who would have been the best in the NFC West had the Rams not moved to St Louis (a valid debate). I had gone out at least once to let them know that this house was poorly insulated, and I could hear everything as if I were sitting right next to them. I also reminded them again we had a seven-a.m. tee time and needed to be packed up to leave straight from the course to head home. I wasn't shocked when I got a response of, "Okay, Dad…"

It sounded like they finally turned in (or just got really quiet) around one a.m. Thank God. Time to get some sleep. Somewhere around three a.m. I was awakened again to more shouting and I couldn't help but channel my grandfather as I thought,

"What the Sam-hell???"

I ripped off the sheets in frustration and went out to the kitchen, finding it weird that the lights were out. Then another shout startled me, and I noticed that someone was lying in a fetal position on the bar-height kitchen table made from wood. Without being able to get a decent look, my first inclination was that Grimey had sleepwalked out here and settled in on some high accommodations to finish out his slumber. Hearing tales about sleepwalkers and how dangerous it can be to wake one, I thought better of it but still wasn't sure it was him. Instead, I went to his bedroom for confirmation and opened the door and there he was, nice and cozy, snoring away.

Uh oh.

Did we lock the door? None of us thought to check what was assumed to be an auto-locking front door as, again, we were in a decent neighborhood. As a result, a local tweaker (which was quite common in Indio - the home of the Coachella Music Festival) had rolled in drunk and stoned looking for some shut-eye. I hurried down the hallway, popped my head into Cliffy's room, and said "Hey, someone's in the house, get out here!"

Cliffy jumped up in spry fashion and said, "Call the cops! I'll go take a look." As we headed out to the kitchen, I dialed 911 and started talking to the operator.

Cliffy was more suited for the action seeing as how he worked out regularly and watched the Ultimate Fighting Championships (UFC) on a regular basis. In stark contrast, with all the injuries, I now just play golf, watch golf, and do twelve-ounce curls… while watching golf…so, yeah, I took one step back.

GO GET HIM, CLIFFY!

Next, I heard a booming voice say, "Hey, wake up! You're in the wrong house, man!"

Upon waking from his high-perched wooden bunk that had accommodated our game of Portuguese dice just hours ago, the tweaker became belligerent and started yelling. It quickly escalated to the point where we were now backing up and looking for weapons or anything to defend ourselves with. We still could not tell if this dude had any weapons on his person, so as he started coming at us, shouting hysterically, Cliffy found an ironing board, used it as a shield/barricade, and tried to corral him back down the hall and away from the master bedroom. It wasn't working.

I sidestepped into my room and attempted to shut the door so I could hear the operator over the shouting. This only pissed him off more and I saw that hand come through the door (no $hit just like the movies!) as he tried forcing his way inside. I had to use all my weight to get the door shut again and get the 911 lady our address. Once that was done, I said, "Just get out here now!" then hung up and proceeded back out into the hall-way to give Cliffy some backup.

Upon hearing the commotion, Grimey (the pit bull of our group) came out, barged right between me and Cliffy and said, "What the hell is going on??? Who the hell is this guy?" It kinda surprised all of us, to be frank! But then I remembered the stories of him and his two brothers growing up in Sacramento and just beating the hell out of each other for fun. Because of that, he feared no man.

GO GET HIM GRIMEY!

No joke, Grimey went to work taking control and shouting at the intruder. "Look, buddy, you need to grab your $hit and get the hell out! NOW!! JUST GO!!" Pretty impressive, really – no arguing, no alternate course of action. Finally, the tweaker be-gan to realize that he might just be in the wrong house and, with a look of confusion, backed down.

Like in most action movies, the cops showed up just as the ma-jor action came to an end and hauled him off, but there were some touch-and-go moments that could have gotten ugly. In the end, we felt lucky to escape with only a story to tell our buddies, but the weekend trip was chalked up to a failure. I definitely learned my lesson. No more golf trips for a while.

Okay, in my defense this wasn't a golf trip. But, for my last and final blunder, I give you…

The Masterds.

If you're thinking, *Don't you mean the Masters?* Well, you'd be partially right. Do we have sanctioned tournament status? No. Is this an actual round of golf? No. Does it resemble golf in general? Sorta!

Back when Covid struck, the Masters tournament was postponed. Just like that, my friends and I had been robbed of our favorite time of year, our favorite golf tournament on TV, and my favorite welcome of "Greetings, friends" from Jim Nance. What could we do? Sit on the couch and watch the previous year again? No way. So, like any group of dudes in crisis, we turned to the internet for a solution and bought the last available bits of golf practice equipment (foam golf balls, collapsible full-size pins with flags, et cetera) and built our own little Amen corner to do Mr. Nance proud. As for the name, maybe not so much.

At this point, I feel I must say something with regard to the name. In case you're wondering, I certainly mean no disrespect toward the Masters or its namesake in any way. As mentioned, it is my favorite part of the professional golf calendar and I love it with all my heart. I have yet to find any of my friends having the same dedication and love in watching each and every round (yes, including the par-3 contest) from beginning to end.

The name I had come up with is merely a play on words because this was a public park and people don't always pick up after their pets. Therefore, there were a few steaming, dog-made hazards waiting out there for us that became part of the game…and hence part of the name. In fact, the first hole is named "Roscoe's Alley" in tribute to a black Labrador retriever who was often left to wander in stealth and do his business at five a.m. each day while his owner got ready for work. The door was simply left open for him so he could set out the hazards for the morning rounds like any greenskeeper might do by moving a hole location or the tee blocks. The rule at the Masterds was always to "play it as it lies," so if you happened to land in close proximity to one of Roscoe's hazards, your next shot might end up being s#*ttier than you possibly imagined. There you have it: The Masterds.

This small park directly across the street from my house, with its assortment of trees, picnic tables, knolly hills, elevation changes, et cetera, was perfectly suited for our half-assed attempt to simulate our own Masters experience – all without leaving the neighborhood. As fate would have it, the layout of the park I had visited daily for twenty-two years, walked my dogs and raised my children on, enabled a good-enough representation of Amen corner with a par 4 dogleg left and a downhill par 3, followed by a par 5 dogleg left, just like the real Magilla. The three-hole layout was a thing of beauty in the shape of a horseshoe surrounding a playground filled with sand, play equipment, and tiny shelters. These were all in the play of course and the surrounding sidewalk even became a hazard of its own that we called "Rays Sidewalk" in honor of Rays Creek – the famous water feature that lines the real Amen Corner at Augusta.

Once the venue was set up, it was determined that we would play early-morning rounds to avoid any run-ins with people in the park or play areas as even though these were foam balls, we were still swinging clubs and maybe having a Masters mimosa (or three). But, rest assured, we'd have full run of the place at seven a.m. Not a toddler, jogger, or dog walker in sight. And so, we played.

Three rounds of three holes for a full nine-hole tournament

would be the setup, and without the ability to mow greens to putting length, or even put in real holes, we stuck the flags in the ground and decided that one club only – the pitching wedge – would be allowed to play your round. With makeshift tee boxes marked by solo cups filled with sand, the goal was simply to hit the flagstick in as few strokes as possible. We had a blast. We had so much fun with this little Covid-induced event that we decided we would use it as a way to celebrate the Masters when it returned in the spring and continue with it each year.

Indeed, the anticipation was building as the Masters – both the real and fake ones – approached in the spring of 2022. We decided we'd play the Masterds on Saturday morning as a precursor to plopping ourselves down on the couch to watch the real Masters with salty snacks chased by beers the rest of the day. However, on this day, we were about to find out that not everyone liked our little production…and find out we did.

Did I mention we all dressed like idiots for this little event? Sorry, I must have glazed over that. But it's easily one of the best parts of the Masterds. Yes, we were easy to spot with our overly-indulgent golf attire of bright colors, fake plus fours (where we rolled our ridiculous pants into even more ridiculous socks - sorry, Payne Stewart), and ladies' visors. Cliffy even wore a bathrobe the first year!

We had finished the first six holes and were enjoying our mimosas at the halfway house (which looks a lot like my driveway), and here it came: a sheriff's cruiser coming up the street. As he pulled up to a stop and rolled down the window, he just looked at us like he couldn't understand what was going on.

Can't imagine why - I mean, four grown men enjoying a cocktail at seven-thirty in the morning…in their driveway…after six holes of make-believe golf…dressed like buffoons. What could he want with us?

"Morning, guys," he said, "We got a report of some people drinking coffee or…tea…in the park…while playing golf… You wouldn't happen to know anything about this, would you?"

You could tell he was annoyed at having to come out and deal with whatever it was he was looking at, but while he tried to be serious – and treat it like something serious – he couldn't help but smile.

"Oh yeah," one of us replied, "that was us…coffee and tea… won't happen again, sir."

He pulled his sunglasses down onto his nose and gave us a wry smile. "Yeah…just take all that booze you have there on the table back into the garage if you wouldn't mind."

"Oh, that? Yes, of course, sir," we replied.

He drove off smiling, shaking his head.

Deputy Dominic France and I have been friends ever since and we talk regularly about town matters like kids on e-bikes terrorizing the city and other fun events. Go figure. It was funny but also made the event kind of a fail. I couldn't believe one of my neighbors or a park-goer had ratted us out! The nerve! Don't they know the majesty and honor of the Masterds? I may have just answered my own question. I guess we'll always have the story to tell, but it really put a damper on our final three holes. Wait, what? Did you think we were going to stop the Masterds mid-round? No way! It's tradition, and we finished like the somewhat honorable pros we are.

After the last year of these wacky, unsuccessful attempts at redemption, it seemed the gods of the mountain, the links (real or Masterds-based), and life in general, had a zone defense going and I needed something big to come my way. This trip Alan had brought up a while back might just be it. While being a long shot, it hung in the back of my mind, surfacing from time to time but dismissed just as quickly as too logistically ridiculous to be possible.

So, what to do after banging my head and hitting proverbial shots of life into the rough for the past year...? You guessed it; I was done. I finally decided to take a break and play sideways out into the fairway of life. and hope that better options would present themselves. No more planning...anything.

A Lot to Think About...Again... In Mere Seconds.

On May 1, 2022. I was at the orthopedic surgeon, who was evaluating me for surgery on my neck. It was getting better with mobility, but I still had no feeling in my thumb and index finger, both of which felt "asleep" all the time (and still do). As it turns out, he was also a nutty mountain-biker with a mild black eye from his last trip down the same damn trail I crashed on. The situation just dripped with irony as I described my crash from a few months back.

"Oh, yeah," he said, "I know the Boneyard."

Unreal.

We shared stories, after which a C5-C6 and C6-C7 disc replacement was the unfortunate prognosis.

Great. Just great.

I was driving home, plagued by thoughts of the impending recovery and layoff time from golf, when the phone rang. It was

Alan. I hit the hands-free button on the steering wheel.

"What's up, man?" I answered.

"Hey, Erik, one of our guys just bailed due to Covid protocols so there's an opening for the trip! You know, the one we talked about back in August...and I need to know if you want in...like ASAP."

As mentioned when I talked about the crash, it's amazing what goes through the mind in a matter of mere seconds. Now, my inner dialogue was going something like this:

My daughter leaving for a pricey college in Florida at the exact same time...sixteen-year-old son would be home alone...nine rounds...I've never played more than three in a row...would the body hold up?...neck surgery is scheduled for June 3....Covid is still a thing...vacation with the wife scheduled in the fall would probably have to be canceled.

Let me break the wall and ask you, the reader, how long do you think it took me to decide to go??? Answer: about as long as it took to read that sentence. Only a few more seconds went by as I continued arguing with myself and processing answers to the list.

Okay, we saved up for college...I've trained my son to be self-reliant and responsible...I'll resort to any modality or medication necessary to get me through a trip like that...I can live with the current numbness in my left hand...I guess Covid is pretty much a cold now...I am married to a woman who will understand.

Alan's still talking, so I cut him off. "Let me double-check everything, but I want in."

The timing was impeccable, with two majorly opposing decisions presented to me within minutes of one another. I had just been working my butt off for weeks, going to rehab, expecting nothing, thinking nothing, and here it was, that proverbial open shot at something special I'd been waiting for. And I'd be lying if I said it was that easy a decision because I knew it was something my wife and I would decide together, but she'd never let me down before.

When I got home, I brought it up as tactfully as I could. True to form, and within minutes, she said,

"Babe, you need this…you've needed it for a while…we'll make it work…you gotta go."

I hugged her, said "You're amazing…thanks, babe," and that was it.

Strategery

July 10, 2022. We're one month out from what we were now calling the "Rota," which was short for the fact that we were playing courses in the Royal and Ancient Open Championship "Rotation."

Alan had set up a group text for the eight of us so we could begin preparing. The text strings had been flying back and forth for days now as a Q&A around the trip but quickly became decorated with hilarious memes and photos (mostly around Roz's low testosterone). But most of it was about the weather, and for good reason.

You always hope for the best weather on any vacation, but with the UK you expect and prepare for rain, or worse. Remarkably, the weather app on my phone was showing eighty to eighty-five degrees Fahrenheit for the first half of the trip, but then seventies and showers for the second half. We could hardly believe the first part, nor would we complain about the second. That rain would not only be welcome and give us the full UK golf experience but would also be WORSHIPED by an overwhelmed and overheated population of the English, Welsh, and Scots.

Over the past few weeks, the news had been full of stories showing London's atmospheric radiator overheating, with days in the nineties and even reaching a hundred. Fires had broken out with no water to fight them. Trains and other services were being shut down due to infrastructure concerns, including the possibility of the steel in the tracks melting! From our perspective, California-like weather looked almost too good to be true, but we agreed to pack for heavy rain just in case. What's the saying - "Better to have it and not need it than need it and not have it"? I think that's right.

As we got closer and the final texts were rolling in, the conversation shifted to the gamesmanship (betting) and it was decided that the money games among the fellas would be twofold throughout the trip. The first game would be a two-man, best ball. In this game, you would be given a partner and the lower of the two scores on each hole (minus any strokes you would get from your handicap) would be counted and totaled. In a twist, these teams were to be blind, meaning you wouldn't know who your partner was until after the round when it was randomly picked. The best ball-winning team would win twenty dollars each, with second winning ten.

The other game was a "skins" game. Ah yes, this is where the real money could be made. Skins is an individual game where the winner of a hole is declared when you beat all players for that hole with a net score (including handicap). The catch was that the win had to be outright, meaning many would tie on the holes creating fewer skins. The total buy-in for both games was four hundred dollars a player for all rounds played.

With $3200 in the pot and only $480 going to team play, that meant there would be $2720 left for skins. That's a decent chunk of change, and one often wonders how much they can win or win back. The best strategy I've found when gambling at golf is to just pay up, shut up, and forget about it like you never had it. Consider that money gone and anything that comes back is just a bonus 'cause the more you think about it while playing, the less seems to return.

So, with all the details set, bags packed, and the money on the line, it was time to go. But, for the Columbo fans out there (yeah, I'm dating myself), I'll say, "Oh, but there's just one last thing…" and that is:

Caddies.

Looping in Caddies
(pun intended)

A month before departure an email came in from our tour operator at Perry golf (I can't recommend their services enough) asking for our caddie preferences for the courses. You really only have two options: 1. The full caddie - and it is what it implies: the full caddie carries for you and only you, except in some cases, when he'll carry for two golfers (if capable and wants to earn double); and 2. The forecaddie. The forecaddie's job is to give some advice to his golfers (however many there may be) at the tee box and then run up ahead as a spotter. The forecaddie will give you a line on which to hit your ball when the fairway cannot be seen and, most importantly, help you find it once it lands. It's difficult to put enough emphasis on that last point. Finding your ball can be most important when wanting to continue golfing! I jest, but losing a ball is just plain frustrating and out in links land; there are so many blind shots you best have a spotter to locate your shot to avoid multiple lost balls and ensuing two shot penalties.

For me it's more than that, as I really enjoy the personality side of the caddie experience. Granted, I had only had two real caddies in my life – once at the Old Course at St. Andrews with Dad, and another time at a little track called Cypress Point Club while playing with Grimey. By the way, Cypress is heaven on Earth for a golfer, and I could write another book on that place alone…but I digress.

During my trip to St. Andrews with my dad back in 2014, we decided to save a few bucks and forego the caddies on all but one course. By the time we did get caddies at the Old (which was the final crescendo of our adventure), we realized what a mistake we'd made. And, ironically, we had both read a book by Oliver Horowitz called *An American Caddie in Scotland* just weeks before in preparation.

A gift from my sister when she had heard I was taking our dad on a pilgrimage to the home of golf, this book was full of great stories and the inside track on the little-known caddie culture in Scotland. For us, it served as a kind of a guidebook to not only watch out for the secret signals and language they used while looping (another name for caddies doing their thing), but also for the incredibly lovely and quaint town of St. Andrews that is filled with pubs, restaurants, churches, and ruins dating back hundreds of years.

Again, the choice to be frugal on the caddie front was a poor one, mostly because they can be as much (or more!) a part of the experience as the round itself. As it so happened, Oliver Horowitz was caddying in the group in front of us. I asked via proxy if he wouldn't mind waiting after his loop, so I could simply thank him for being such a big part of our trip. He obliged and met us in the pub and proceeded to tell us some other great stories not mentioned in the book. Most interesting was that he had now gotten so famous he was not only the most requested caddie at St. Andrews, but also flown via private jet around the world to just to tell his stories.

The power of a simple book.

As for the caddies Dad and I got at the Old Course that day, well, this is worth a mention.

Per instructions from our tour service, Golf Scotland, we met just outside and in front of the Royal and Ancient Golf Club overlooking the first tee. Waiting there for us was our guide Mark, ready to introduce us to our caddies. I had drawn a man named Davey. Standing about five-seven with brown hair, a goatee and glasses, he seemed nothing like some of the characters Oliver described in his book. In fact, he looked quite normal. You might say I was almost disappointed! He introduced himself pointedly and asked me which way I liked to shape the ball; and by this, he meant which way, if any, I liked to curve the ball when hitting. My feeling of disappointment vanished immediately. I told him I usually played a fade (a ball that goes gently from left to right for a right-handed golfer), to which he responded, "Aye, good answer, lad." From that response, it was obvious which way this course bent around the dunes from tee to green and his years of experience would guide us appropriately. I liked this guy.

Davey was perfect throughout the entire round – he found just about every single ball I hit sideways (and I was sure to tip him accordingly) – but he was not nearly as memorable as his counterpart, and my father's caddie, Jimmy. When it came to expected caddie-quirkiness, Jimmy had enough to cover both he and Davey for the entire round...and then some.

Had any one of us met Jimmy on the streets of St Andrews, we would have been puzzled at the proposition that he does two to three loops a day at a place that was considered a royal treasure. He just didn't look the part. But, after reading Oliver's book, maybe he did. As round as he was tall, with tattoos fore and aft on leg and arm (and God knows where else), he gave the impression he'd been a bit of a hellraiser for most of his life. I'd go as far as to say he might have ridden a loud chopper or two with ape hanger bars and leather chaps in his day. As he was wearing a hat you couldn't see much hair, but hello, what's this? A thin wisp peeking out from the back? Not long enough to be rubber-banded as a ponytail, it was simply a curly tail of white hair. As he took his cap off to wipe his brow before we set off, we noticed a full-on, white mohawk (thinning but decent, nonetheless), bringing the whole persona into the picture. Even more curious was this looper's tattoo of the Grim Reaper on his left calf. It looked like it had lost a lot of detail over the years as tattoos do, and I imagined Jimmy had dodged the full-sized version of the Reaper quite often throughout his life.

Now, being a caddie at golf's most sacred cathedral, you would think communication to be paramount in success with your client and maybe even a requirement. Jimmy, however, spoke Gaelic-Scottish with a tongue and accent so thick my poor father could barely understand him. I didn't believe Dad that it was that bad until I heard Jimmy read a putt somewhere around the 4th or 5th hole.

"Wat ya a ta doo far dis poott dis fooking loong is ta plae it wheeeeey oot heyr and lit it teeke tha breek aboot heyr, an witch it foonel doon to tha hoole."

WHAT? It was obvious us Yanks were no longer in Kansas.

Okaaaaay, can we get a translator down here?

Jimmy left such an impression in my mind that I couldn't help but attempt my first real prose since college, describing the scene on a Facebook post for all my friends back home who were following our trip. Accompanied by a photo of the man, the myth, the legend, the description of Jimmy on my social media page went like this:

***

This was my dad's caddie, Jimmy. If I didn't know better, I'd have sworn this guy came straight out of the shire from the Lord of the Rings. A stout, round, tattooed, hobbit of a man with a grisly attitude and a penchant for cursing in heavy Gaelic, my dad couldn't understand much of what he said but I don't think it would have mattered. His poor ankles were so swollen they looked like tree trunks stuffed into cushy socks and overloaded ASIC Gel running shoes. He really didn't even walk as he carried my father's bag. Instead, he just keeled from side to side on knees that no longer bent, like a small tugboat fighting the waves at sea with a broken rudder. Good Ole' Jimmy.

***

Even after reading Oliver's book about this place and its people, this caddie business became more interesting than anything I'd seen on or off the course during our trip. It was a spectacle of sight and sound, and Jimmy was a prime example. When I asked Davey mid-round how Jimmy could do it, he just said,

"Yeah, old Jimmy's been at this so long now we don't know how he does it; he's got grandchildren… who are driving! But we all know he's coming to the end." Then he asked, "Do you see all those mounds out here alongside the fairway?"

I turned to look in that direction. "Sure."

"Well, all the boys around the caddie shack talk about it all the time and think that when that day comes, he'll just wander out onto the course and just become one of them. No fuss at all."

"Sounds like a movie to me, " I replied, "and a damned good one!"

In fact, that's Field of Dreams stuff right there…

I was fascinated by the caddie life: an honest day's pay for an honest day's work – mostly. Stories Davey told us of good tippers were good, but the stories of the bad ones, though unfortunate, were more interesting. St. Andrews was no bargain. Prices had gone through the roof over the years (if you could even get a tee time) so you would figure the tips would be high as well. Not so. Davey shared short stories about wealthy magnates of industry, elite athletes, and stars of the screen and I was absolutely shocked to hear how often caddies were stiffed when Sean Silver Screen or Johnny Football played a sh*tty round. It was downright upsetting. But all in all, they stuck with it. These guys would gladly strap on a bag, take on forty-mile-per-hour head winds, suffer the rain, and get stiffed on a tip, rather than spend one day sitting behind a desk like the rest of us schmoes.

Over the past ten years, there have been several books and documentaries written and filmed in St Andrews to describe this strange subculture that lies within the world's most famous golfing venue. Bill Murry (Gunga Galunga!) has narrated one of the best, called *Looper - The Caddie's Long Walk*. I simply can't recommend this enough.

However, none of them, whether on screen or paper, do it the justice it deserves; so, like most things, to fully understand a discipline, event, or occupation, one needs to roll up their sleeves and simply partake in the experience.

And so I did.

I caddied.

Teeing Up for Later

Just out of college in '95, I got a job working at a driving range/golf shop called Roger Dunn at the Islands. It was there I met a police officer from the City of Orange named Joe Zorola. Joe lived close by and had wandered in to check out the latest golf gear we had in stock while on duty. We struck up a conversation around the comparison between the latest offerings of Callaway and TaylorMade. In fact, the conversation was all it was going to be because although the customers could test any club they wanted, Joe couldn't possibly swing a club due to a forty-pound officer's belt/small arsenal topped by a bulletproof vest. So, with that in mind, I started with the small talk; something timely in the news…you know... something trivial to keep the conversation.

"SOOOO…HOW 'BOUT THAT O.J. THING??"

No comment. It had just happened. Too soon, I guess. Back to the story.

Joe would become somewhat of a regular at the shop and we became friends quickly. At one point he notified me that he ran the transportation group for the then-called Nissan Open at Riviera Country Club in Los Angeles. He asked if I had any interest in coming up from Orange County and volunteering, so I did. A fun little gig, my job would be to merely take a Nissan courtesy vehicle and head to the airport to pick up the pros as they flew in from Hawaii following the Sony Open. Some came in on Saturday after missing the cut while others came in on Monday. It goes without saying that those who came in on Saturday were not in as good of a mood as the Monday pickups. My favorite, though, was picking up Ernie Els (on Monday) and his then-girlfriend Leizel from a private jet at Santa Monica Airport and bringing them back to their hotel.

Due to traffic, we had to take a bunch of side streets to get back to the Palisades where Riviera Country Club was waiting. Along the ride, the traffic swelled on the local freeways resulting in our having to detour through the side streets. I jokingly asked them if they had any special requests on the radio since we weren't going to go more than twenty-five miles-per-hour anytime soon through the back streets of Brentwood. Ernie said, "No, but aren't we close to O.J.'s house? Can we go there and check it out?" A bit of a strange request, but I thought, *Why not?* As it turned out, the street was barricaded off due to spectator traffic; however, we were able to peek up the block as we crossed by. Again, I thought the request was kind of odd to say the least, but still, they were super-nice people.

After that drop-off I headed over to LAX to pick up Loren Roberts, Jeff Maggert, and their caddies. It had been at least a year since both Loren and Jeff had played the Ryder Cup at Oak Hill and the US had lost by a single point. While heading back to the course we again hit LA traffic on the 405, slowing down to a swift five miles per hour. It was too late to do anything about it, so, rather than just sitting there listening to the radio, I thought I'd strike up some conversation. Seemed like a great idea.

"I hope you don't mind me asking a question about the Ryder Cup…"

"Not at all," said Loren "We're pretty much over it, right Jeff?"

"You are," said Jeff with a joking sound in his voice.

I could see from the rearview mirror that he appeared cool and neither caddy had a reaction.

Golf, as we all know, is a pretty tame sport but the Ryder Cup is intense. Imagine an NBA-finals-game level of cheering (and jeering) as fans line the fairways ten people deep.

"What's it like to play for your country on that stage?" I asked.

Loren replied, "It's an incredible amount of pressure…"

The group in the car continued talking about how the pressure at the Ryder cup can just destroy even the best players. Kiawah Island 1991 quickly became the focus and Loren talked about one golfer's mental battle to close out a match and how it did just that. Essentially (I'm refraining from mentioning his name out of pure respect and sympathy), this player had the win in hand at four-up in match play and as part of a mental melt-down, shanked his ball into the water on the 17th hole. This was after watching his opponent hit his own ball into the water first!

I could see the mood in the car changing, so I guess I thought I should try and make it worse by saying,

"Soooo, he just choked?"

Insert sound of the needle being pulled off the record.

With that, the car went silent.

My eyes raced up to the rearview mirror to see what all the non-commotion was about. I could see one of the caddie's eyes go wide as he looked across at the other caddie. It was apparent that this word was not used often inside the PGA circle.

Loren just said, "You could never understand, few people could, and if you did, you would never use that word."

Nicely done, Hansen.

I wanted to exit the vehicle but there was nowhere to go. We were stuck in the car and the car was stuck in traffic. I did, at one point though, contemplate getting out and walking. Instead, we just sat there while I tried to think of a way to apologize for even mentioning it. Needless to say, the last few miles just went by quietly.

Some courtesy driver.

They can't all be great stories, I guess, but it gave me a real first look into the seriousness of the mental game of the professional golfer. A look I hope I never see ever again.

Overall, I had a lot of fun experiences from the LA Open, thanks to Joe. Quite often he'd give me a headset and tell me to go walk around or hang out on the putting green with the pros or even a celebrity or two. I will always be thankful for that.

Joe and I kind of lost touch after I left the golf business for technology and had only talked a couple of times in the last ten to fifteen years. It wasn't until two years ago, when I was going through my address book, that I saw his number and decided to reach out and see how he was doing.

He said he had left the LA Open and was now running the caddie shack at the Hoag Classic, which was a Champions tour event (for pros fifty and over) at Newport Beach Country Club. This raised an eyebrow as it was a heck of a lot closer to home than LA was and sounded like fun.

"Yeah, we just got done with the last one," he said, "but do you wanna caddie in the Pro-Am next year around March?"

"Heck, yeah!"

"Great, we pay a hundred dollars per round, and you'll do two rounds per day. You'll caddie for two guys…and any tips you make are yours…so at the very least it's four hundred. It's rain or shine, no matter what, and you get to meet the pros like Fred Couples, John Daly, Vijay Singh, and it's pretty fun!

Hmmm…rain or shine…okay… rain…carrying bags…busted up body…rain again…

Being a movie junkie, I immediately conjured up images of Bill Murray as Carl Spackler in *Caddyshack,* hoofing for the reverend in a hurricane, uphill, both ways.

This is Southern California dummy, it never rains… just do it.

"Okay, I'm in!" I said.

"Okay, we'll talk in a few months as we get closer to the event. See ya."

"No problem, man, I won't let you down!"

Out of Our Comfort Zone, We Go...

Now, those who know me would agree that I tend to overdo things when I get excited about some new hobby or adventure. As the tourney grew closer and the anticipation built up, I began researching everything caddie-like. "What makes a good caddie" was what I entered in the Google search bar. "What is a caddie supposed to do" was another entry. I got back varying answers, of course, and I'd seen plenty on TV, but the gist of it seemed to be:

1. Carrying the bag – duh. The hardest part. *Next.*

2. Checking yardage and handing your player the right club. *Okay, I have a rangefinder/scope and know the game.*

3. Washing the club after use – *makes sense.*

4. ...and the ball when needed – *of course, okay.*

5. Raking the traps – *I love this part…it can be so Zen-like.*

6. Help reading the greens – *hmmm…maybe we get one of those books like the guys on TV have? Probably not.* I'm no pro at reading greens, but I imagine if your player makes putts (which is where the money is made at a team event) he might be more inclined to tip well. *Okay, I'll figure it out.*

Next up came the training. Carrying the bag was a foregone conclusion, but I hadn't carried a bag and walked a course in years. YEARS, I'm telling you. I'm the fattest skinniest guy I know and now that I've cut out mountain biking and turned to golf, the situation isn't getting any better. In fact, my favorite joke (by Dmitry Martin) about my fitness lately is, "Yeah, I work out religiously – that's twice a year and around the holidays."

As for golf these days, all I do is drive a cart around on Saturday and hit a ball as few times as possible. So yeah, I'll need to get in shape for this thing. I decided to start carrying my own bag when I play my back nine Sunday rounds and then maybe I'll progress to eighteen holes later. And then, somehow, thirty-six to get ready for the Pro-Am.

Turns out walking was a nice change of pace (even nicer than I thought it would be) and I started to realize how much I missed the pure essence it adds to the course and the experience. There's a real peace of mind to it. Why did I walk so much back when I was young and suddenly quit? I tried to remember.

Oh yeah, not only were carts for the rich and lazy, but when I started golfing back in the last century, golf carts looked and drove like an abomination of engineering.

Built like a hovercraft from the atomic age, the original golf cart had three wheels, a flat, awkward triangle mounted in the middle of the dash as a steering wheel, no cup holders, and no roof. With this design, it seemed like they tried to make the cart experience so bad that you *wanted* to walk. Today's carts have leather bucket seats, GPS, eight cup holders, cell phone chargers, ice coolers, and yes, even Bluetooth speakers to connect your phone to. Like a home entertainment system on the course, it just screams, "Never mind you're out in nature on a beautiful day… let's just get fat." I may sound old, but I'll say it: I've come to realize that this experiment that is the American golf cart (yes, American, we invented it in Beechwater, Florida) has slowly detached us from what can be a wonderful combination of golfer and terrain, along with the walk toward a better round and slimmer waistline. But I digress.

As I walked more and more rounds, I became comfortable with the fact that I could carry for at least nine, if not eighteen, holes. And Newport Beach CC was a fairly flat course so thirty-six could certainly be in the cards. I was feeling stronger and healthier, and with my common knowledge of the game, I could easily do items two through five on my googled checklist with utmost confidence. Still, I couldn't help feeling that I could be doing more to cover all the bases. I'm sure Joe had all the answers I needed but I didn't want to bug him with questions. Since I didn't want to let him down either, I came up with some questions (you know…the kind you ask without actually asking them) so I wouldn't sound so dumb. I dialed his number.

"Hey, buddy, just calling to check in."

"What's up?" he said.

"I was just wondering…do we have to carry both the golfers' bags while we walk with all their stuff in them, or do they transfer them to a lighter bag?"

"Carry the bags??? You know you guys don't actually carry them, right??

Um, I do now.

"Oh, yeah, yeah, of course not," I replied.

He's now sensing I had it all wrong. And I did. He went on,

"Yeah, the caddies are going to just hop on the back of the cart and ride along from shot to shot and you hop off and hand them their clubs and give them yardage and so on…you get the picture. You'll sometimes even drive the cart up for them as the players like to walk with and talk with their pro; after all, that's what they pay the big bucks for – to hang with their pro."

"Oh yeah, that makes sense…"

"There may be a situation," he added, "where there's a downpour and carts aren't allowed onto the course and we have to carry bags, but that's only happened once in the past ten years or so and for, like, half a day. You're all good man, talk to you later."

Whew! No carrying! This is going to be easy!

Now all that was left on my checklist was reading greens. I would venture to say that I'm a decent putter so it stands to reason that I can read a green or two, especially at my local courses where I've played a lot and learned the secrets. More applicable, though, I had also played Newport Beach CC a couple of times at charity events with good buddy Alan and made my share of "Bombs," or long putts, while contending in the scramble play. But I knew that's not pure green reading so I wondered how I could get a leg up and do some research on these greens beforehand. If only I had a man on the inside…

Enter Brian Horn.

Brian was a former customer-turned-friend I met back in '99. We played a few rounds together but mostly kept in touch over text for the past twenty years, always talking about playing but never getting it on the books. Still, our conversations were always fun, and I knew he was a member at Newport Beach CC; and, as luck would have it, he also sat on the board for the Hoag Hospital Charity Foundation and the Tournament itself! It all seemed to be coming together for some reason.

Standing a robust five-foot-ten, this dark-haired, bearded guy had been a former multisport athlete (football, basketball, surfing, et cetera) but had been sidelined from the game of golf having sustained injuries that would have landed most mortals in a wheelchair. You'd never know it, though. Always with a smile, a handshake, and a hearty laugh to boot, it was hard to not have a great time with him, even if just for a brief chat.

I reached out to Brian and asked if I might be able to come out, take a quick tour of the course, and roll some balls across the greens to get a read while taking some notes to complete my self-imposed training. Without missing a beat, he replied:

"That would be awesome…I'd love to help out…come the weekend before and we'll get out early before the members hit the course and we'll check 'em out!"

Awesome. Just awesome. I am truly blessed.

It was now Sunday, the week before the tourney. As I arrived at Newport Beach CC, the sun was coming up over the adjacent homes lining the course, casting a golden hue across the property and through the fans of sprinkler water blanketing the fairways. The best players over fifty from around the world would be coming into town as Newport Beach is one of the favorite Tour stops on the schedule.

I headed into the clubhouse where Brian was waiting to grab some coffee and breakfast. During our meal, he told me how he was almost back to swinging a golf club… after having his entire spine fused by a metal exoskeleton. Wait, what?

This can't be true…this guy sitting right across from me?? Comfortably?"

He saw the incredulous look on my face and decided it best to show me a picture of his X-ray. I haven't included one in the book, but try to imagine a metal spine on top of and connected to a human spine almost top to bottom. Then came a pic of the scar and now I'm done with breakfast.

"Good lord, man! How is that possible?" I asked.

"Modern science, man," Brian replied.

For the rest of the morning, Brian and I hustled around in a golf cart, stopping at each green, rolling a few balls here and there. I got some great insight from him on the slopes and drainage points as I drew pictures and lines with arrows of each break and its associated speed in my pocket-sized notebook. Along the way, Brian would stop to say hello to every greens-keeper we ran into, which counters any notion of the stereo-typical stuffy or snooty country club member anyone could possibly have. The grounds people work proud amounts of overtime in preparation for an event like this and the charity raises millions, so why not thank every person who makes it special? After we're done, I thank Brian for a fun and informative morning and tell him I'll catch up with him on Wednesday when the Pro-Am starts.

Fake It...
'Til You Can Make It

It wasn't until I walked onto the grounds at six a.m. that I reminded myself that I wasn't a morning person. But guess who was?

John Daly.

Good 'ole JD had a reputation for going late most nights at the pub, so I was shocked to see that he had beaten me (and most everyone else) to the course and was practicing on the putting green all alone. Watching him, I realized again that the Champions Tour still meant a lot to these players. Though no longer on the PGA tour, JD was there to make money and knew that each hour of practice, pro-a.m. or not, might yield a larger piece of the two-million-dollar purse. As I walked on by, a thought crept into my mind that maybe I had been naïve, and that maybe…just maybe…JD never went to bed at all.

As I walked over to the caddie tent adjacent to the range, I noticed some of the caddies had also beaten me there and were now congregating. You could hear and feel the excitement from some about being reunited after a serious tournament dry spell a la Covid. These guys were exactly as I had pictured them as I remembered St Andrews and the tales of Oliver Horowitz. Caddies were a special breed, and the most interesting of examples were often the drinkers, smokers, gamblers, and scrappers all in one. This assorted band of golf gypsies continued to show up in all makes and models, sizes and shapes, colors and creeds. Some looked like they had not lived the most sheltered lives...no, far from it. They were hard workers; and you could see on their weathered faces their many battles with the Pagan gods of the sun, the wind, the rain, and the earth.

I tried to blend in as best I could, and managed to eavesdrop on stories of who (and, more importantly, who not) to caddie for at these events, so when the time came to get our assignments, I would be as attentive as possible. I hoped I didn't get one of the guys who had been the negative subject of those caddie conversations – one of whom, mentioned above, was hitting balls just outside the ten about twenty feet away.

I was still feeling a little uncomfortable, so my strategy was to seek out an innocuous-looking fellow and ask for some advice. Looking the part with the white sun hat (popular with golfers and caddies looking to avoid skin cancer), sleek Oakley sunglasses perched on the brim, and towel thrown over the shoulder, Kirk Mashburn was definitely the guy. He was even eating fruit rather than the supplied breakfast sandwich of egg, bread, and meat-flavored substance. The final selling point to me had to be the shoes. Too funky to be an accident, HOKA shoes were apparently the footwear of choice for caddies, for as I looked down to see Kirk's I noticed several others were sporting them as well. Looking like a running shoe on the upper part, the bottom had a base or platform at least three times the size of a normal shoe. It was almost comical, but the HOKAs were built for purpose and, as I came to find out, the caddies swore by them.

With the appearance of multiple educated decisions from head to toe, I introduced myself to Kirk and asked if he had any tips for a first-timer like me. He was gracious in explaining the basics like raking bunkers, cleaning balls, et cetera, and, more importantly, how to stay ahead of the group by anticipating the next shots and always being ready with a club - even before the player was. We talked for ten minutes or so, and he was a wealth of information having caddied for over fifteen years and multiple pros.

Then, a hush came over the crowd as Joe Zorola, our caddie master, took the highest ground he could find. While looking over his ragtag gathering of loopers, he thanked everyone for coming and welcomed them back after two years of absence.

Joe stood and commanded the scene (no doubt from his training as a cop) and laid down the rules. He'd been doing this a long time and had too many stories to share about caddies going beyond their duties, forgetting their job and place in the golfer/caddie equation. Some had fallen victim to the all-too-tantalizing invites from their groups to have a drink, or a shot, or ten, and then maybe try and hit a golf ball. Some caddies had been banned and Joe made sure to mention it. The fun and enjoyment took a back seat to the fact that he had a job to do, and we were all part of it. The goal was to do our job well and nothing else. Be a pro and you will get invited back. "F" it up and you'll be asked to leave, or worse, get escorted off the grounds. It had happened at the last tournament, and by the looks on the faces around me most of the caddies remembered it. Names were whispered with some uncertainty, but the point was made.

Formalities and responsibilities addressed, the excitement mounted as we picked up our assigned morning foursome and saw who our pro was. There were two caddies per foursome, along with the pro and his own caddie for the morning and then we'd get a whole new group for the afternoon. I would be teamed with another caddie named Mike for the next two days, and we drew pros Paul Goydos for the morning and Jay Haas in the afternoon. Excellent. Both had reputations for being fantastic guys and great players, but Paul and I attended the same college, and I wondered if we'd have a chance to talk about it if given the time. After a brief intro and armed only with our range finders, divot repair tools (and my little green reading book), Mike and I donned our standard-issue bibs and ran to our assigned carts to meet our group.

The morning group was an interesting bunch; the owner of a staffing company and local restaurant had purchased this foursome for his son and himself along with his senior guys who ran the operations and the finances. I wouldn't know it now, but I'd be caddying for them in the afternoon the next day as well. Mike ended up getting the father and son team and I got the two senior guys - the first of which we'll call "Golfer No.1." Golfer No.1, a good-looking guy of average size and physique, carried a handicap of two. He also had a nice demeanor and we hit it off immediately.

The other guy…I couldn't quite put my finger on. He intro-duced himself well enough, but, it did seem there was a bit of a chip on the shoulder. "Golfer No.2" stood about my height – six-foot-two – but skinnier, with a Gomer Pyle posture, hat brim tortured into a half circle, and a dip of skoal firmly packed into his lower lip. Golfer No.2 is the guy who motivated me to use this naming convention, and you'll see why in just a bit.

The morning started well, and I went to my preparation early, but it was difficult to find a rhythm. I managed to keep up and help my twosome by giving yardages per shot and cleaning equipment. Mike also seemed to be a beginner at caddying and was asking me a few questions here and there as if I somehow knew what I was doing. He must have seen the little book I pulled out from green to green to help my guys out.

Golfer No.1 was more than happy to listen to my reads on putts; however, Golfer No.2 would hear me out with a frown and then draw his conclusions as if he knew better. It wasn't long before missed shots and putts for bogey led to mounting frustration, but he kept his cool for the most part. After five or six holes Golfer No.1 and I locked in for some precise reads and putts for two birdies, which built a little excitement. The course was far from difficult, with few trees or hazards to con-tend with, so the only real defense Newport could throw at a player were these tiny, firm greens. Because of this, my little book was working, and the others were taking notice. Our pro, Paul Goydos, was not having much luck with his drives or ap-proaches but man could he putt. With a reverse standard grip he "rolled the rock" with utmost precision, making putts from all over. Unfortunately, he was only making pars when the team needed birdies from him in this best-ball format.

On our back nine, Golfer No.1 and I got in a rhythm of our own and felt like a real team as we followed yardages, proper landing areas for rollout, risk-reward scenarios for good pars, and a couple more birdies. Golfer No.2 hung in there but was not having his best game, and I couldn't help thinking his attitude was a big part of it.

It's no coincidence that the word golf has four letters in it. One of my favorite quips is the fact that it's only called "golf" because when it was invented all the other four-letter words were taken. Golfer No.2 has already used a few of them. However, despite his terrible mood, I continued to help and be a pro because you just never know when the right word of encouragement or piece of advice might turn things around. In turn, it might also yield a better result when the time for tips came.

Mike's father-son team was an absolute treat to play with and they netted some good holes of their own, but I took today's first round as validation that the preparation with Brian just a few days before resulted in a good round for at least one of my golfers, and that was enough.

After the round, Golfer No.1 immediately tipped me with a smile and generous offering as we parted ways, but Golfer No.2... had vanished.

Stiffed? As you recall, I'd heard about this from Davey in Scotland, but on my first round?

Damn.

But stick around. This story is far from over.

Due to a "shotgun start" (where everyone starts at the same time but on different holes), we found ourselves back on the 13th hole, and halfway across the course as we finished the first round. As a result, by the time we drove all the way back to the clubhouse to meet up with our second loop, we had no time for lunch. Unbeknownst to me, Mike had stopped and gotten in line at the volunteer lunch tent for our free, caddie-level af- fair. I, on the other hand, rushed to find our afternoon group, who was already waiting in their carts ready to depart.

Uh oh, am I on my own? Is Mike coming back? I guess I'll have to figure this out!

As I mentioned earlier, Jay Haas was the pro in our afternoon group and was joined by his son, Jay Jr, as his caddie. I was extra excited to meet Jay Haas simply because of his reputation as a great player and even better person. Gracious as expected on the first tee, he introduced himself and his son and shook hands with each player as if he'd known them for years. I met my golfers, who all appeared to be in the life insurance game from the "Pacific Life" designations written on their cart signs. I explained to the group that my coworker would be delayed due to some confusion around the lunch situation, but not to worry – even as *I* worried about the thought of double-timing this loop for God-knows-how-long. However, I also saw the opportunity to pick my golfers; and hopefully, the next Golfer No. 1 and maybe a better Golfer No. 2.

Sitting in the cart comfortably while the others stretched out on the tee box, he looked a solid six-foot-two, with brown hair parted in the middle and round, Harry-Potter-like glasses. He wore tastefully chosen yet unassuming color-neutral golf attire, and had an air about him that said, "I'm a solid business guy." That, coupled with the higher ratio of woods-to-irons in his golf bag, told me all I needed to know.

I thought to myself:

These other three guys look like low-handicappers and can probably manage their games. This guy looks like he works hard and spends more time in the office than any of them. He might be the host of this group and probably doesn't have time to play much, and a good round today might just yield a solid showing for both of us. Yup, he's the guy.

This was immediately validated after I introduced myself.

"Hi," I said, reaching out for a handshake, "my name's Erik and I'll be your caddie today, how are you?"

He reciprocated the shake and replied,

"Hey, Erik, I'm Chris. Good to meet you! ... Look, I need you to know that I'm the worst golfer here with a fourteen handicap, and I stubbed my toe so bad last night that I considered canceling. So, unfortunately, I won't be doing much walking and need the cart, but I'm happy to drive you around to each shot if that's cool."

Yup, he's my guy! This is going to be fun...

I don't know if it was the haste of the situation or my light-headedness from missing a lunch (and now a co-worker), but I unconsciously blurted out, "Hey Chris, no problem at all. I used to teach the game here and there and I did a bit of research on the course, so with that handicap of yours and my little research book here (I held my and Brian's work up proudly), we might just hole some putts and make you the hero of this thing."

"I'll do my best," he said.

Hmmmm...maybe I'll get a chance to get a little coaching in here and there...

Chris' playing partner, Joel, was a good guy and player (and a little demanding), so between the two there was enough work to go around. Still, Chris and I did our best to cover the entire foursome's needs, driving all over creation so I could give yardages, rake traps, and read greens for everyone for the first few holes. Luckily, I found that the other two players, Josh and Joey, were both a zero (scratch) handicap and didn't need much attention. Chris was struggling a bit off the tee with his disability but on the second hole managed to string a couple of shots together and get it on the green in three after a topped three-wood followed by a decent chip to twenty-five feet.

"Two putts for bogey with a stroke gets us a net par here, Chris," I told him.

With the rest of his team putting for pars but with no strokes, this was the first chance for a small victory for Chris from a makeable distance. I gave him a quick read and then scrambled over excitedly with my little book to give Joel a read. Before I got over there, I was waved off as he turned his back and asked Jay Haas, the pro, for his advice instead. Should I be miffed?

Let's see, thirty-three wins across the PGA and Champions tours versus rookie caddie Erik Hansen on his first day... Nope, no offense taken, Joel. In fact, I wanna know what Jay thinks too!

I'll spare you the suspense. Joel hit a bad putt and it wouldn't have gone in if God had given him the read. But Chris made his. Net birdie for Chris. Net birdie for team Pac Life!

Two holes later, my counterpart Mike showed up on a cart, having bummed a ride from one of the tournament officials, and handed me a granola bar. Chris saw me happily inhaling it and said,

"Hey, Erik, I've got a whole box lunch in there if you want it...we all ate lunch before the round...grab whatever you want!"

Now I'm more motivated than ever to make him a hero.

The rest of the day went pretty well, though I tried to give Joel another read and he missed it. From that point on he only wanted advice from Jay Haas, and I was fine with that. You can't win 'em all.

As Chris and I rode along he talked about his position as manager at Pacific Life for over fifteen years.

Intrigued, I said to him, "Hey, I know like one person who works at your company, and I haven't talked to him for a long time...I doubt you know him...but figured I'd ask...his name is Tim Breland."

"Oh, Tim works for me."

I just about fell out of the cart.

"Seriously??? Tim and I have known each other for thirty years and had some good times, but it all went silent when he and his wife separated... I miss that guy! We even look alike!

"You're right," Chris replied, "He does kinda look like you... he'll be here tomorrow entertaining our second foursome so you can see him then...Maybe you can even caddie for him. It's his fiftieth birthday today!"

My mind raced back to when I last saw Tim.

"Wait, he's fifty?? Today?? The last time I saw him was on his fortieth birthday...so it's been ten years to the day! That's unreal."

I exhaled, my mind reeling as I thought about the sequence of events that led me here. The thought of surprising ole Timmy B was almost too much to imagine, but I texted caddie master Joe immediately to see if I could get into his group. His lovely wife, who happened to be covering for him, responded with:

"Hey Erik, this is Lesley, I'll have to move some stuff around, but I think we can make it happen."

Super excited. I couldn't wait to tell my wife and dad, both of whom knew Tim well. They would never believe this!

Like any golfer, Chris made an assortment of good and bad shots that day, but none of us could have predicted his play on the 15th hole. The 15th was an uphill par 5, and he managed to hit two shots of good distance to end up in the bunker about fifty yards short of the green. After dropping him off with his wedge, I drove the cart around the side of the green and as he limped and nestled down into the bunker in preparation, he hesitated, backed off the ball, and asked me, "Hey, how do I hit this shot anyway?"

I replied, "Two main things to think about. First is the swing; just put the ball back in your stance, choke up on the club, take a three-quarter backswing and accelerate through it..."

"What's the second thing?" he asked.

"Actually, I'll tell you the second thing after you hit it."

"Okay," he said, "here goes."

Without pause and on cue, he took it back to seventy-five percent, then proceeded to hit it out perfectly to about twelve feet, where he was now putting for birdie but with a stroke(!)...for net eagle. His group cheered.

"Shot of the day, Chris!" shouted Jay Haas.

As I reached out and extended the rake to him to help him out of the bunker, he asked, "What was the other thing?"

"Hardest shot in golf," I said.

Jay heard my comment and echoed it aloud because, as every golfer knows, the long bunker shot is darn near impossible to hit the right distance let alone anywhere near the hole. Unfortunately, where his ball ended up on the green was darn near unmakeable; on top of a two-foot shelf that rose above the hole, about ten feet away and, as a result, there was simply no way to stop it or putt it close. Chris would understandably miss his birdie-net-eagle but end up with a par-net-birdie for the best score in the foursome. He was standing tall. We both were.

As we ended our round Chris extended his hand and offered me the most gracious of tips; he even invited me to play at his home course down in Carlsbad. We vowed to stay in touch and hoped to see each other again next year at the very least.

My first rounds as a caddie were done, and I felt great.

Normally, all caddies would hop the shuttle back to the volunteer lot a mile away, but because I knew Brian I was extended an invite to the player's dinner where I would be able to see my afternoon players and embellish on our accomplishments and fun moments.

It was an incredible privilege and an honor, but I was to be there incognito and certainly not as a caddie, as this would most likely be frowned upon by Joe and the tournament director. In an attempt to keep a low profile, I put on a jacket that covered my caddie credentials as I hustled upstairs to the dining area. Between the physical exertion and my excitement, I was a bit flushed and overheated, so I unzipped my jacket before helping myself to the buffet. It was a gorgeously appointed affair of carved roast beef, marinated chicken dishes, fancy salads, and delectable desserts, and I could hardly find enough room on my plate for everything I wanted – especially after missing lunch!

Eventually, I found Brian talking with a few of his friends – a mix of players, pros, and members – and sat down next to him. As I began to eat, he subtly curled an index finger at me, then leaned in to whisper something.

Maybe he wanted to introduce me to someone important or let me know something cool.

"Hey, dummy, take your caddie credentials off. The tournament director is sitting right across the table."

$h!t.

There they were, my caddie credentials, around my neck like tiny billboards with bright green sections highlighting that I was not where I should be. What a jerk. Brian was gracious, but I could not help but kick myself in my mental balls. In my defense, the director looked like he was no more than eighteen, but still…

Come on, Hansen…

You would think I had learned my lesson, right? Nope. The following day on the course was even colder and I had on two layers and a jacket, meaning my badges were completely buried. But as we transitioned from cold golf course to warm dining room, layers came off…and yup – there they were again. Brian just looked at me and shook his head.

I'm a moron. He might not ever talk to me again and I wouldn't blame him.

Shocked that he didn't ask me to take the bus home immediately, I went on to enjoy the dinner that first night and listen as the winners were announced. I was pleasantly shocked to hear that my afternoon team had won in a card-off (where you settle a tie by looking at the scorecard and taking the best score from a certain hole or set of holes). With all my caddying responsibilities, I had no idea what the scores were in our group, let alone the rest of the field throughout the day. I was really focused on Chris' play and excited about surprising a long-lost friend come early morning. In the end, we didn't know for sure which hole won the card-off, but Chris's playing partners all suggested it was his score on fifteen that settled it.

The surprise reunion in the morning round with my old buddy Tim was as fun and special as I hoped it would be. The look on his face when I walked up and told him I was his caddie was hilarious. We hugged it out and struggled to comprehend the odds of this happening. And the thought of me being his caddie was just as great as I knew his game to a tee and he knew I knew it. I felt that with his wedge game, coupled with my green reading experience after two rounds, we had a chance to go low and win the Thursday flights. But Mother Nature had other plans, and the wind picked up and the skies darkened as a chilly storm system came into town from the north.

Regardless, we would enjoy the round by catching up on old times, and I don't think I could have wiped the smile off my face if I tried.

The pro in this group was Mike Weir. As a golfer, Weir had a few things that made him stand out. The first was that he was from Canada (nothing wrong with that, eh?) Second, he was a lefty and one of the few on the PGA to ever win. Last, but most importantly, he stood about five-foot-nine, weighed in at a trim one-hundred-fifty pounds, and – even at fifty – looked like he was about twenty-five. Despite having a few cards stacked against him, he had become the first left-handed player to win The Masters in 2003 and was one of only four to ever win a major. He had solidified his place in golf history and demanded the respect of so many. The dude could flat-out play and I was looking forward to watching it.

Back to Tim and me and our random (but fated) reunion. For the first few holes he was hitting it as well as ever but was unable to make any putts. On the 10th hole, he had a short wedge shot from the fairway after a good drive and, because of the chilly conditions, this smaller-than-normal green was like hitting a turtle shell. With made-up caddie confidence, and in a voice akin to something that I'd heard on TV, I called out my proposed strategy.

"Okay, so this green is hard and fast and slopes to the back and we're going straight downwind. And there's nothing behind the green but a large downward slope that could take you into the shrubs at the bottom, and that's bogey or double. I think we hit it high so it lands soft about five yards short and rolls onto the middle. Hit your sixty (degree wedge) about fifty-five yards and that should get it done."

He turned and looked at me and asked,

"How many times have you done this now anyway…??"

"The caddie thing?" I asked.

"Yeah."

"Well, including yesterday's rounds…twice, I guess."

"'Cause you sound amazing!" he joked.

Laughing, I told him I had been "faking it until I could make it" since yesterday and he joked again I should think about quitting my job. Now that was hilarious…I'm no pro, nor did I need a career change, but it sounded like all the prep was worth it to this point.

For reference, the "fake it/make it" thing was something I'd learned and adopted into my life since I attended a little league umpire clinic held by a guy named Brian Beckner back around 2015. Brian (another friend and golfing buddy) from the first uttered word, explained that these little league kids were all playing the game; they didn't care what you did. The parents, on the other hand… well, they could be cold-blooded savages. They seemed to think they could call a ball or strike or even make a safe/out call from thirty yards away. Brian said I should never, ever show fear and always fake it like I knew more than they did because even after just one clinic, I probably did.

This lesson was something I've leaned on quite a lot since then. Whenever I did something new, I remembered to act like I knew what I was doing even when I didn't, because, dang it, most people wouldn't know the difference.

As we finished what would be a lackluster round by Tim's standards (even in the wind), I came to find that although I would have done this for free, Tim was no slouch in the gratuity department and his partner followed suit, making for another successful round.

The Moment of
(a) Character

I'm glad you hung in there for my last caddie round at the Hoag (and most likely for the year until it came around again), as it ended with an unexpected twist. As mentioned, I had drawn the same group Thursday afternoon that I had in the morning the day before, but with a new pro – Sandy Lyle.

I was looking forward to seeing Golfer No.1 again, but Golfer No.2 (if it weren't already obvious), not so much. I hadn't forgotten about the absence of a tip the day before, but I still had a job to do. A funny thing happened, though: as I walked up with a chipper attitude, I heard Golfer No.2 groaning about losing the first day's tournament in a card-off to another team.

Whoops. I know who they're talking about…and you know what? I'm good with it.

Not surprisingly, this had already set Golfer No.2 into a bit of a pre-round tailspin. By his reasoning, there's no way another team could have beaten them. Come to find out that while they didn't get the first-place trophy, they did get the same prizes valued at somewhere between five hundred and a thousand dollars! Still, he wasn't happy, and this, coupled with the lack of the tip, made me wonder again if this was going to go well between us. Honestly, I thought that maybe he just forgot to tip me, but I certainly couldn't bring it up.

We headed off to our first tee box, which was number sixteen in our shotgun. All players but one found the fairway and in no time flat, Golfer No.2 turned to curse words when I notified him that his ball was right up against one of the few dwarf palms on the course. This gave him no option but to hit out sideways – which he did…poorly. Ironically, on this same hole the day before he had hooked his drive in the other direction off the tee, hitting a condo, and immediately tossing a club across the fairway. This hole appeared to be his nemesis and would continue to hang over his head mentally for the rest of the round as the weather and his play took turns for the worst. But nothing, and I mean nothing, would prepare me for what I experienced on our 16th hole so close to the end of the round.

That cold, windy storm had arrived and it had already put a major damper on most of this round. Large swirls of gray replaced the once-blue skies and layers of clothing would be added by those smart enough to bring them. Understandably, no one in the group was playing well as the cold bonded muscles and bones into one.

Our 16th hole of the shotgun was the 10th, which headed straight out from the clubhouse and ran down alongside the range and adjacent to the 7th green, which faced back to our tee box. There had been some trees planted there for some sort of protection, but though it did obscure the view of the green it was not the shield the greenskeepers were hoping for and we were about to find out why.

Father and son hit their drives well enough, as did Golfer No.1. Golfer No.2, however, took a hefty swing but came completely over the top, producing a wickedly shoved slice down the right toward that 7ᵗʰ green. A few of us shouted "FOOORE!!!" as loud as we could and hoped the wind would carry our warning cry faster than the ball could get there.

There was not much we could see beyond the smallish trees standing guard and there was no commotion, so Mike and I jumped in our carts and headed out to find the balls. The one furthest right would be the most challenging and I'd hoped no one had been in the vicinity when Golfer No.2's white-dimpled projectile came flying through the area.

As I pulled up around the trees that had blocked us, I saw that play had stopped and a group of people was gathered around a golf cart beside the green. My heart sank as I knew immediately that the ball must have hit someone; then again, no one was on the ground either. I took some measure of comfort in this as I continued up to the cart while everyone looked at me with confusion, as in, "How could you do this?"

I asked the first person I came upon if the ball had hit someone, to which they replied,

"Oh yeah, and you got her good…She's over here in the cart."

As I came to a stop, I saw a woman sitting upright (thank God)

with a bloody cloth being held up to her face by none other than Corey Pavin. Turns out that as she was putting out, the ball had hit her right on the cheekbone, splitting it open about three inches. Considering that the eye lies a half-inch above the cheek and the temple just above that, it was a miracle she wasn't blinded, knocked out, or worse. Relieved to see her conscious, I apologized and explained that we yelled as loud as we could, but even Corey said, "With this wind, it wouldn't have mattered."

Thanks, man, I honestly feel a little better.

I phoned Joe Zorola at the tent but again got Lesley, who sent the medic cart out. It came remarkably fast but, to our shock, continued down the 10th fairway and out of sight. Another call to Lesley would have them turn around. I couldn't help but think:

Note to the medic team: get to know the course better - much better. Someone's life just might depend on it!

We waited for Golfer No.2 to arrive so he could see what had happened and make sure she was okay.

"There's my player over there," I said.

To my surprise, with hands in his pockets, he walked to the edge of the 10th fairway, looked in our direction for a second or two, then turned around and kept on walking.

I didn't know what to say. Corey just looked at me and gave a shoulder shrug. Of course, whenever you enter a golf course you assume the risk of being hit by an errant ball… but still. Once the medics arrived and took over, and after my fifth apology, I drove off to rejoin my group. Yet I just couldn't stop thinking about the reaction and the seemingly non-compassionate way in which it was handled. When I caught up with my group on the green, I walked over to Golfer No.2 and let him know she was going to be okay, and he thanked me. And that was that.

We finished up our round in the wind as best we could, with balls being sprayed this way and that and shots into the wind being met with a helping of dirt or sand we didn't ask for. When we finished up, Golfers 1&2 ended up tipping me for the round and thanking me for my help with the situation. It was obvious he felt bad and just didn't know how to handle it.

Despite the unfortunate ending, my caddie time at the Hoag was everything I hoped it would be and more. It reinforced the fact that preparation is the key to success (and even more so in first-time situations). It had made the two days more enjoyable with every little victory. I also walked away, already looking forward to next year – as well as with a pocket full of money for two days of work. Most importantly, I now had some skins money for England!

To bring this full circle, when the question from our group organizer at Perry Golf was put forth regarding caddies, I replied, "Give me a caddie at each of the Royal Courses!"

Bring on those Royal characters! I can't wait!

My Home of Golf

If you read the quirky chapter list of this fine literary master-piece and have now made it all the way to this point thinking, *Oh boy, here comes the obligatory tribute to St. Andrews,* well, you'd be wrong. While the Old Course is considered by many to be the "Home of Golf" and akin to the Vatican in its cathedral-like setting and thousand-year-old history, it is not *my* Home of Golf. No, my Home is more suited to my strange sense of humor and ridiculous ability to remember forty-year-old movie quotes (yet somehow manage to forget anything my wife tells me). No, my Home of Golf is a more of a nuthouse, really – and that nuthouse is:

Bushwood Country Club.

Now, as those who share my passion for movies will know, Bushwood CC is home to arguably the finest movie on the game of golf: *Caddyshack.* As it turns out, that magical course where the movie was filmed still exists in Davie, Florida, about thirty minutes from my yearly vacation spot of Lauderdale by the Sea. How perfect. Things are starting to come around.

Somewhere between an intercoastal tour of Fort Lauderdale

(where they filmed the pool and boating scenes) and the boredom-induced poolside research of the local courses, I managed to locate the hallowed ground of Bushwood Country Club (CC). It was now called Grande Oaks Country Club and, according to the reviews, was a fantastic course to play. My research continued.

The story of this course – which incidentally had undergone a name change (from Rolling Hills CC) and several redesigns since the filming of *Caddyshack* – was that it was chosen for the movie primarily for something that it *didn't* have: palm trees. The screenplay was written in part by Brian Doyle-Murray (Bill Murray's brother) and based on a local course in Winnetka, Illinois called Indian Hills Club. All the Murrays had grown up on this course, caddying and playing golf as they honed a razor-sharp wit and glorious sense of humor that would serve them well to this day. Once the movie was greenlighted, rookie director Harold Ramis (who later went on to direct *Vacation* and *Groundhog Day* and star in *Ghostbusters*) needed a golf course. He began looking for a course that resembled Brian's Oak tree-lined Midwest club but could also provide more amenable weather for which to shoot the movie. Hello Florida…hello, Grande Oaks. The rest was history.

Having learned this, I now had a new golf goal in life; to play Bushwood. No matter the cost, no matter the name change, and no matter that it was private, I would find a way. Silly, you say? Maybe. But I can tell you there are those out there who share my affliction and understand the importance. After all, if you were between the ages of eight and fifteen when this movie came out, it could be as culturally formative to you as any movie you ever saw.

A proverbial "slobs vs. snobs" scenario, it had everything from a coming-of-age story of caddie Danny Noonan (Michael O'Keefe) to a disapproving and snooty Judge Smails (Ted Knight), an obnoxious real estate developer Al Czervik (Rodney Dangerfield), the Playboy Ty Webb (Chevy Chase) and the assistant groundskeeper, Carl Spackler (Bill Murray). It was a tour de force combo of classic and comedic actors and future stars who went on to feature in some of the funniest movies and tv shows ever made. Even the gopher achieved acclaim and can still be found on top of almost any golf bag with a driver up its butt as a headcover.

And, last, but certainly not least, who could forget the judge's niece, Lacey Underall (Cindy Morgan). I can't remember if this was the first R-rated movie I ever saw (I was nine years old), but hers were definitely the first "movie boobs" I ever saw. Billy Martin (if you've been paying attention, I almost killed his grandma) and I watched that movie until the VCR damn near broke. The rewind button was most certainly worn out. I remember the first time said jumblies came across the screen followed by, "Wait, wait. Go back!! Go back!!"

It's one of those movies where, even though you have the DVD in the player ready to go, and it comes on TV, you'll just proceed to watch it, regardless of the commercials. Why? Probably because it just came to you with no effort and it just happened. Like some sort of kismet.

Not that Lacey was the sole reason, but it's the movie I've seen the most, period. Maybe fifty to sixty times. Yeah, maybe I'm sick.

But I'm not alone.

To most people, though, the movie might best be known for a legendary battle between groundskeeper Carl and the furry little gopher. Now, the battle scenes between the two were probably fake (chuckle), but the blowing up of sections of Rolling Hills CC for the movie was anything but. In the '80s, before CGI (and even Jerry Bruckheimer), when you wanted something to explode, you literally blew it up. As the filming of the movie was coming to a close, the crazed partied-out cast members were ready to blow this place up as was written in the script, but there was one small problem: the owners wouldn't approve it. Therefore, in a clandestine plan, the production team lured the course ownership offsite for a sit-down about filming the scene, during which, you guessed it, they blew up the course. The explosion was heard for miles and was even reported to the local police and airport control tower as a possible plane crash. Spoiler alert: the gopher lived.

A rite of passage for hacker and pro alike, the movie Caddyshack has transcended golf courses to the workplace water coolers and halls of fraternity houses ever since. While most women found it eye-rollingly ridiculous, it was something that almost any man could relate to and if you ever ran across a golfer who proclaimed, "You know…I've never watched it," you knew he was either a liar (he'd seen it and forgotten it) or he was no *real* golfer. It's quite simply a part of the game.

With my new lofty goals set to play this sacred place, I began reaching out in every direction I could think of… but to no avail. So, having learned my lesson about forcing the situation, I decided to play sideways on this one. I even told my dad that

I had given up for now while catching up on the phone. He said he wished he knew someone and could help out. And that was it.

Weeks went by and then, during another call with him, it happened. Apparently, he mentioned it to his long-time friend and former customer Tom Vaughn, who lived close by the course in Davey and was an avid golfer. As luck would have it, Tom had a vendor who belonged to Grande Oaks and set up a time for when Dad and I would be back there for vacation in July. I went nuts. Call me crazy, but I was as excited as the day when I heard my buddy Grimey had gotten us on Cypress Point Club in Monterey. Now that I think about it, that was pretty crazy.

Unfortunately, when July came Dad had to back out, but his friend Tom would come and pick me up at my hotel in Lauderdale by the Sea for our afternoon round. Yes, you heard that right, afternoon golf, in July, in South Florida...a veritable sauna. No problem, though, as we Caddyshackers all know "the good Lord would never disrupt the greatest round of my life!" Yes, I would play Bushwood, no matter what.

It had been at least fifteen years since I last saw Tom, but to me he still resembled a tall Kenny Rogers with silver hair and a neat beard to match. After a harrowing ride with Tom through Fort Lauderdale traffic (we got some nice air over the train tracks well before the gates came down – thanks for warning me, Dad), we crossed into the town of Davie. As we got close, I remembered the bike ride that Danny Noonan took on his way to work through all the high-end homes in Bushwood

Estates as the movie began. The Kenny Loggins song "I'm Alright" started to play in my head, but was then followed by that sound of the needle being pulled off the record... as there were no homes leading our way in!!

Ah, the movies. That scene was obviously shot in some other gated community far away (probably in Illinois to maintain the illusion that they were still in the Midwest). With that, I thought maybe it was best to temper my lofty expectations for the rest of the day as we turned off down a busy road next to a strip mall and up to a sturdy-looking gate amongst the trees. Tom passed muster for entry with a shout of our names and tee times into the small, black, elevated speaker box, and we found ourselves heading up a short, oak-covered driveway.

And there it was...the clubhouse.

The sounds of Kenny Loggins started up again but then faded into angels singing as rays of sun passed through the giant trees and reflected off the hood of Tom's Cadillac.

I'm home.

I recognized parts of it immediately but noticed that other parts were missing. It suddenly became apparent that there were at least two clubhouses where they shot the movie which, again, speaks to the "movie magic." However, there was no mistaking the covered drive-up and valet stand, where my movie mind remembered Spalding throwing up into the sunroof of a perfectly good Porsche, Carl shooting out the lantern while Ty and Lacy spoke about "skinny skiing," and Al Czervik pulling up in his right-hand drive, convertible Rolls Royce and yelling out to his sidekick, "Wang, what's with the pictures…? It's a parking lot!"

I am most definitely home!

While Tom put his shoes on by the car, I dashed up the steps and into the clubhouse. I felt like a kid running through the gates at Disneyland with nothing but a Ziploc bag with tees and a glove I'd brought in my suitcase. Oh, and I almost forgot – I also brought the authentic orange Bushwood CC caddie hat I had bought for my Danny Noonan Halloween costume years earlier where no one knew who I was (except my golfing bros…shocker.)

Clubs? No, I decided not to lug my clubs on and off the plane for this one round as Tom was gracious enough to set up some loaners through his buddy we were playing with. I noticed them waiting conveniently for me at the valet stand as I rushed past and into the front doors.

The clubhouse was beautiful and tasteful, and you could tell that although the club would never escape the fame, they did their best to obscure it; probably for the sake of members looking to have a golfing experience of their own identity- and independent of the film.

I had forgotten a belt, so I went off to the pro shop. While it wasn't completely filled with Bushwood gear, there was a section dedicated to my brethren who came to play Bushwood and not Grande Oaks. And, wouldn't you know it, they had a very nice, overpriced, undersized, Bushwood CC logo belt with gopher heads and all waiting just for me. While there were plenty of other belts available, I would suck in my gut and make this one work down to the last hole.

As I walked out of the shop toward the first tee, I spied a very special shrine within my Mecca just off to my left. It was a flower bed, and it was full of beautiful mums.

In the original screenplay there was a scene that showed a sweaty, inebriated assistant greenskeeper Carl (Bill Murray) hitting the tops off flowers with a grass whip. Harold Ramis, however, as the director, had something else in mind. He asked Bill if he ever imagined he was winning a race or event or something similar and if he could conjure up some dialogue along with the action.

Bill replied, "Yeah, yeah, yeah, say no more; I got it!"

For those reading who are true disciples of the religion of Caddyshack, let us recite from script and good book of Assistant Greenskeeper Carl Note: for the full effect you must slur the words while contorting your lips-high left and low right (as if you're stoned to the bejesus):

What an incredible Cinderella story. This unknown comes outta nowhere to lead the pack at Augusta. He's at the final hole. He's about four hundred and fifty-five yards away, he's gonna hit about a two iron, I think ... (Carl reels back and swats the head off of a mum. Petals fly like confetti.) *Boy, he got all of that. The crowd is standing on its feet here at Augusta. The normally reserved Augusta crowd is going wild ...* (He pauses as he notices some golfers coming) *for this young Cin-*

derella who's come out of nowhere. He's got about three hundred and fifty yards left. He's going to hit about a five iron… it looks like, don't you think? (Carl pulls the grass whip back to demolish the next mum.) *He's got a beautiful backswing … That's … Oh! He got all of that one! He's gotta be pleased with that. The crowd is just on its feet here. He's a Cinderella boy, tears in his eyes, I guess, as he lines up this last shot. And he's got about a hundred and ninety-five yards left, and he's got a, it looks like he's got about an eight iron. This crowd has gone deadly silent. Cinderella story, out of nowhere, former greenskeeper, now about to become the Masters champion.* (Carl reels back one last time and — Swat! — blasts the third mum to smithereens). *It looks like a mirac – It's in the hole! IT'S IN THE HOLE!!!*

This scene brought golf out into the mainstream, much to the delight of cut-off jean, half-shirt, tube sock-wearing, blue-collar workers everywhere; and conversely to the chagrin of course managers trying to maintain a respectable golf club anywhere. With no back story, and certainly no reason, an underachieving assistant greenskeeper stood in a perfectly good flower bed and hacked the heads out of the most innocent and adorable of plants – and coined at least a dozen catchphrases. As a testament, as I write this, I'm watching the Chiefs vs. Bengals on TV and, unbelievably, a commercial pops up starring Tony Romo as Carl Spackler(!) hitting mums from the same spot while reciting the speech! Yes, the fact that the former QB of The Dallas Cowboys ("America's Team") was paying homage to this moment proves my point. It was *that* brilliant, and as I stood there staring down at said flower bed, I wondered, should I ask if I could maybe whack a mum? It would really add to the experience…hmm…

"Let's go, man! Before it gets really hot!"

I was snapped out of my dream sequence by Tom and his two buddies down on the putting green.

They must be joking,

It was ninety-five degrees with ninety percent humidity and, not two feet out of the lovely air-conditioned pro shop, I'm dripping sweat and wondering if there's some way I could take the a/c with me.

"Sorry! Just taking it in!" I replied.

I hadn't played golf with Tom for at least twenty years, but Dad had reminded me how he liked to play quickly and in a no-nonsense manner once he teed off. He also prided himself on finding golf balls – so much so that he pulled me some near-new Titleist Pro-V1 x's from his garage stash of somewhere near a million balls. Given this, I knew I might be driving alone at times from tee box to green as he searched the tall grass periphery on his ball-hawking safari.

Tom had knee problems that plagued him late in life. As a result, many shots around the green were hit with one hand on the hitting club and the other hand on another club as a crutch to hold himself up. He had gotten pretty good at his one-handed wedges. The problem would come when Tom hit off the tee with no crutch to lean on, and my dad had told me to watch out for that.

As we started into our round, I continually tried to make reference to landmarks from the movie. It was really difficult to see any holes that vaguely resembled what I had seen so many times on the TV screen (ironically, I've actually never seen it in the theater!). Even after coming home from the trip and watching the movie, there weren't any obvious sightings that I could find. A disappointment? Heck no! The course itself was a blast and a challenge – very well thought out with no two holes looking or playing the same.

Leading up to the 6th hole, I was struggling to find a fairway with my borrowed TaylorMade driver. It was a fine modern club with plenty of technology, but in a case of "It's not the arrow, it's the Indian" (not the club, it's the player), I had been pulling the ball left consistently. This tee shot was no different as I found myself down the left side again and essentially jailed in a narrow corridor of skinny oak trees. This corridor extended about seventy yards down the left with two, thicker trees at the end doing a good job to block any exit. There was an opening just to the right, about five yards wide between, and at the end of the corridor that made the green visible, but it was a ridiculous shot. To top it off, I still had another seventy to eighty yards beyond this opening to a green that bordered a lake on the right with the hole tucked all the way in the back. What to do… what to do. The go-for-it shot would require a very low, punch-fade (because I think we'd all agree a punchy-slice would be too much) off a packed sandy lie with no margin for error. Playing out sideways was surely the more prudent of plays, but somewhere in my overheated brain I felt myself thinking of Carl Spackler hitting those mums. If he could pull off shots of three hundred and fifty yards with nothing but a five-iron, why not me? My brain was obviously melted.

Okay, then…come on, Erik…you got this…

Cinderella Story…outta nowhere…with an impossible shot and everything in the line here at Bushwood… He's got about a hundred and sixty to the flag…looks like he's got about a choke-down three-iron…he's got the ball back in his stance…wanting to keep it low…beautiful backswing…

Whack!!! ssssssssssss… Knock!!!

Oh, $h!t.

As solid as I had hit anything all day, this punchy three-iron stayed plenty low; but darn if it didn't stay dead straight. As it hit the largest oak seventy yards down the corridor dead center, I waited for it to take a direction left or right (leaving the property or heading for the lake). But though I heard the noise, I saw no movement either way. In a split second, I saw the ball get bigger and bigger in the window as it came straight back at me. My instincts scrambled and mixed the signals to my brain sending my legs to the right while my head ducked left. However, in that instant, my brain also calculated *inertia x velocity x distance x bull$h!t=something* and somehow understood it would run out of gas before hitting me squarely on my person. So, I stayed frozen in my footprints, waiting for something to happen. As the ball lost speed, it somehow came seventy yards straight back and settled right into, you guessed it, my shallow sandy divot.

With a snort of disbelief and a silly grin, I looked around to see if anyone had seen this. I mean, I had been playing this game for a long time and I had never seen this. Turned out no one else had either as Tom was off on his usual hunt to find golf balls and the others had their hands full playing the hole their own way. But here I was again, facing the same darn shot.

Enter Golfer B.

Now, as every seasoned golfer knows, there are two golfers inside each and every one of us: Golfer A, and Golfer B. The Golfer A persona (your first attempted and wildly unsuccessful shot) is a knock-kneed, uncoordinated, confidence-lacking, perfectionist, whose handicap is feasibly at least ten shots worse than Golfer B.

In stark contrast, Golfer B (your second ball, make-up shot, mulligan, do over, et cetera) could go pro whenever he wanted. He's an ace.

To further elaborate, Golfer A shows up to the tee box looking over-focused, nervous, and constipated, in non-matching gear, tightly-packed and ill-fitting, while Golfer B shows up with a cocktail in hand, having just bombed the men's room on the way to the tee and wearing white-on-white with the collar turned up and Ray Ban Wayfarers (picture Don Johnson in *Miami Vice*). He gets all the girls, drives a Porsche, and, most importantly, drives the golf ball straight down the middle every time – that is, of course, as long as he goes second.

My point is that, in golf, your second, do-over shot is almost always ten times better than your first; in fact, this is so well known in the golfing community that this naming convention carries other monikers like "That Second Guy"; "Second Team – All American," and my favorite: "Golfers Middle Name."

Mine's Carl. Honestly. That's the "C" in Erik C. Hansen and, I'm proud to say, my grandfather's name. I find it ironic that it's also the same name as the sweaty, gopher-battling assistant greenskeeper from *Caddyshack*.

And speaking of the gopher, I kept my eye out at Bushwood but failed to witness any brethren or relatives of the furry little troublemaker who starred in the movie out on these links. If there were, they were laughing their butts off at that last shot I'd just hit. But I digress…where were we?

Oh yes. Was Bushwood taunting me? Daring me? Daring Golfer B? Because he was up to bat now. Golfer A headed to the men's room after that last attempt. No matter, having shifting personas, Golfer B was armed and prepared with a club in hand and ready to prove he was the man that Golfer A, never could be.

In a relaxed state, having seen the mistake in the technique that Golfer A had just demonstrated, Golfer B (Carl) stepped up and hit the shot to perfection. It hissed with both sidespin and backspin, curving through the hallway of trees, passed the big oak, landed just on the front of the green, and funneled all the way back to the hole to about two feet. A gimme par. Damn, he's good. I'm glad to have him on my bipolar twosome. There you have it: Golfer B explained, in not-so-short order.

As for Tom, he had done well to get this far on hobbled knees and clubs for crutches. However, on the 8th hole tee shot, as he came through the ball, his knee gave out with a pop and he let out a scream that, had it been uttered by anyone else, would have conveyed to the group, "I'm done!" Not Tom… no, he simply popped it back in place somehow and continued to play.

As we turned for the back nine, we were now in the longest part of the day and the heat. A small savior came in the form of a breeze that kicked up for moments at a time, but whenever that breeze died down, it got so bad *my sweat* would start to perspire. By the 14th hole, I was dunking my hat in the ice cooler (now mostly ice water) and just putting it on my head for immediate relief. How do pros do this for days in a row on the tour?

We were somehow surviving it and, best of all, my game was coming around. I birdied 15 and 17 and as we came up to 18, I was even on the back nine. The 18th hole was a stunning surprise with a forced carry over a lake with a gorgeous, lone oak tree in the center standing on its own little island. A picturesque, slowly arching bridge carried you over and past it to the fairway. Before we teed off, Tom asked me what green I wanted to play: the one on the left over the water on approach, or straight ahead? A choice of greens to go for? This was something I'd never seen before! Maybe it was the greenskeepers' idea to give the oak-covered 18th hole a chance to rest and recover. Or, maybe it was this way to truly torment those needing a par. Either way, it was an interesting option that could play a major role in any match that came down to the 18th.

We collectively decided to play straight down the middle to the easy green and not over the water as our brains were well-done from the heat and none of us needed any further challenges. As a result of our conservative decision, we all made pars for a fun finish. The birdies coming in netted me an even back nine of

36, giving me an 80 at Bushwood and I was more than happy with that.

I was starting to feel fully recovered from my injuries and my tempo and timing were coming back. I couldn't help but think that I was trending in the right direction with my game just in time for the summer match play at my club, and, more importantly, my upcoming trip to England.

We finished up with lunch and some beers and I took a final trip to the pro shop to overheat my credit card and conclude the awesome experience at Bushwood - my Home of Golf.

The Rota Shed-jule
(that's Brit for Schedule)

August 10th- Flight to London

August 11th- Pick up at London Heathrow from Perry Golf- Drive to Kent, play Royal Cinque Ports

August 12th- Royal St. Georges

August 13th- Princes- Himalayas and Shores – travel to South of Wales

August 14th- Royal Porthcawl

August 15th- Travel to Southport, Hike Penny Fan (Brecon's Beacons) and onto Vincent Hotel

August 16th- Royal Lytham and St Annes

August 17th -Formby

August 18th- Royal Birkdale

August 19th- Royal Liverpool

August 20th- Drop off at Manchester Airport (I take the train to London for my flight back out of LHR.

The Yanks Arrive,
One by One

Touchdown in London. As our double-decker Airbus A380 rolled down the tarmac, the pilot notified us that it was sunny and eighty-five degrees. *Are we really in the UK?* With a solid jet stream, I made Heathrow in record time, coming in an hour early. I'd been told by Alan I would fit right in with this group so I couldn't wait to meet them and get acquainted.

I came into the terminal with Chad Roesler right behind me. Chad Roesler (aka "Roz") was a five-foot-ten fella with jokingly low testosterone (per his hilarious texts) from Kansas. He was relatively easy to spot flowing out of customs in the matching University of Kansas hat, pullover, and golf bag, leaving no doubt he was team JayHawk.

We exchanged pleasantries and, in comedic fashion, tried to persuade our way into the Delta One luxury lounge while we waited for the others. After being scoffed at by the desk attendant for only being "Delta Comfort," we retreated downstairs to loiter with "our people" and wait for more of the group to arrive.

More funny texts with selfies announced Conrad Roberts, also known as "Con" or "Dobler" (oddly, after the football player Conrad Dobler). Conrad appeared to be the face of the organization, standing at six feet on the nose, with flowing jet-black hair and a finely manicured and Covid-motivated beard. After a few words were exchanged, I picked his accent to be somewhat Bostonian, but he tells us he's been in the UK for a week visiting relatives. Turned out he's from Wales! The three of us grabbed some pints of Lager from the terminal grocery (a brilliant thing here at Heathrow) and Conrad shared some stories from his trip thus far, including a short hike he did with the family at a place called Brecons Beacons.

Next in was Joe Brotherton, or "Joe Bro" as his golf bag indicated. Seemed everyone's bag had their name on it except mine, and I made a mental note to get that done when back in the States. Joe Bro shared that he just came in from San Diego, where he sold commercial solar energy systems, and we both agreed that the weather was shockingly warmer here than there.

Just as Roz joined in the conversation around solar power, I noticed a guy with a smaller frame, dark curly hair, and a KU golf bag sneaking up behind him. His bag said "Barney" on it and now I was really thinking I needed to get this done locally while on the trip, just so my poor golf bag didn't feel left out.

As "Barney" approached, he gave me a wink and brought one finger to his lips in a shush gesture as not to alert Roz, then jumped right onto his back! Yikes! I couldn't help but think that we were all at the age where such a move might maim a middle-aged guy about to start a golf trip, but Roz looked like a sturdy fellow and didn't even flinch. A handshake and a hug immediately followed, and I assumed that this was their first in-person outing after two years of Covid lockdown. He then came over, shook my hand with utmost enthusiasm, and introduced himself as "Brad Barnett, but people call me Barney." He was hard not to like from the start.

Last, my good buddy Alan arrived and brought over the rest of the crew from the United terminal, and introduced Scott Wilkinson or "Wilk," and Brian "Murph" Murphy, both from Denver. Our group was now complete with Alan, Barney, Roz, Dobler, JoeBro, Wilk, and Murph ready to take on the Old Country. Let's do this.

Now outside the terminal, we met the man who was to be our faithful ward and coach driver, Neil Crukshank. Neil stood about five-ten with neatly buzzed, white hair that came to a point almost military style. It sounded like he hailed from Scotland and had the perfect accent to go with it. He also had a decent tan for a Scot, which I could only assume was gained from waiting around for his passengers while they were out playing the links. He greeted us and helped us load up our luggage and club and then we all fumbled into our well-appointed transport. Neil had picked up some refreshments (mostly beer) so we were able to drink more on the bus while we all got caught up and/or acquainted. It had been a lot of planning and waiting to this point, and now the time was finally here to have a drink and relax. However, we quickly found that rest stops were few and far between. This meant that with each beer and kilometer passed, when the time came to pull over, guys would pile out like it was on fire.

About halfway to our first destination, the anticipation and excitement became palpable. Conversations about the courses and expectations were all over the place. I felt this might be a good time to hand out a little project I had been working on. A favorite hobby of mine is making hats and other logoed/personalized items for friends and family on special occasions. For this outing, I worked with my Mac-based photo editor to create a hat design that looked British (yet somehow still American) and had all the course names listed. I landed on "Rota Trip 2022" as the theme on a British flag, surrounded by the course names, with the final touch: the Open Championship cup in the middle. This design was laser-etched onto a leather patch and sewn to a navy trucker-style hat. Alan and I ordered a dozen and they had been taking up some major space in my suitcase reserved for souvenirs.

As we neared our destination, we made a short, unremarkable speech, then passed them out to the team. We even had one made for Neil. They all loved 'em.

Royal Cinque Ports – Course 1, Day 1

Socked In

As our two-hour shuttle ride south from Heathrow was coming to an end, away went the gorgeous rolling farm-land properties and in came the smaller, seaside two-stories joined by little shops and tiny service stations. The narrow Sandwich roads twisted towards the beach, and there was some tedious negotiating to be done by the driver. Neil did well to ensure our beluga-like transport could get us to the town of Deal, where our first round of golf awaited us. Car after car would come at us and Neil would have to pull over with the roads being just big enough for two small vehicles. Running twenty minutes late, we piled out of the bus and headed for the pro shop like a bunch of Americans about to miss their first royal tee time, which we most certainly were.

***

Founded one hundred and thirty years ago in 1892, Cinque Port's name derives from Deal's membership in an ancient group of trading towns granted special privileges by the medieval English monarchs, known as the Cinque Ports. The course runs along the coast of Sandwich Bay, on the same stretch of coastline as Royal St George's Golf Club and Prince's Golf Club, adjacent to the north.[1]

***

As we checked in, we were surprised to hear that because we were wearing shorts, we had to wear knee-high socks. We were originally told this was required for St. George and that would be it. No matter – this rule has been around a lot longer than us most likely, probably over a hundred years, so best to comply.

In the past year, I've had several people asking what the "story was with the socks" as they browsed through my photos from the trip. There were a few different explanations we came across but surprisingly, nothing definitive from the natives. Some believed it was a way to keep people from showing their hairy gams and that all parts of the leg should always be covered. Others said it was just to protect the legs when searching for balls in the gorse. My favorite version was that it had to do with the longstanding attachment some of the Royal courses had to the military. Since golf attire had no adorning bars, stars, medals, et cetera, the socks became a way to identify a ranking officer. The higher the socks, the higher the rank. The lower the socks, well, you were probably scrubbing toilets (or nowadays carrying someone's golf bag). This explanation made more sense as soon I noticed the caddies wearing bobby socks while

---

[1] "About the Course," March 13, 2023. European Players Tour. https://www.europeanplayerstour.com/t1-royal-cinque-ports/

the players were being forced to wear these socks that looked more like pantyhose. I had packed some calf-high argyles I picked up from a trade show just a few months ago and managed to sneak onto the course without buying a pair. The plan was to wait until tomorrow at St. Georges where I could get some sexy logoed socks to pour my skinny legs into.

After checking in with the starter inside, we sidetracked into the main doors of the ancient clubhouse for the restrooms. We were reminded again by a member to remove our hats while inside the building (another wardrobe convention but still found today in many private courses and clubs).

We grabbed our rental trolleys and headed out to the first tee to divide into our foursomes. I had read in Tom Coyne's book that the James Bond Movie *Goldfinger* was shot somewhere around here as Ian Fleming lived in the area. Coyne also mentioned that Penfold Golf Balls were the ball of choice for the deadly secret agent of the '60s. So, on the side, I devised a little game as had I picked up a dozen Penfolds Hearts, the golf ball that Bond played with back in the day (and, coincidentally, were really hard to find!)

In the movie scene, Bond challenges Goldfinger to an eighteen-hole match and, during the round, catches his audacious nemesis cheating. The nerve! There is also a moment during the round when Bond throws, of all things, a bar of Nazi gold onto the green while Goldfinger is putting out, with the intent to confront his foe and get down to brass tacks. This, to me, is such a funny scene, as if someone would lug around a one-kilo gold bar in their trousers just to make a point. But back to the Penfold Hearts.

As a tribute to Bond and his silly little product placement, I took these non-confirming Penfold Heart balls and distributed one to each member of our group. We would play the par threes with this ball and whoever won the skins with a Penfold, the skin for that hole would double. Not only that, I had also picked up a special prize; two gold bar-shaped, travel-sized, bottles of whiskey. They honestly looked the part. Whoever had the best performance with the Penfolds would win this little trinket. I was probably overdoing things again, but I took one and gave the other to Alan to award to his foursome when a winner was declared. It was hard to get the group to focus on this new side game, which was totally understandable. We were all so excited to play our first round. I also had no sleep on the flight, so I was off too. You'll see why in a moment. Stay tuned.

The first foursome was to be Alan, JoeBro, Dobler, and Murph. Up second would be Wilk, Barney, Ro, and me following behind. There were so many moments leading up to this day when I'd wondered how I'd do with this group of amazing golfers, having only ever played with Alan before.

Just don't make a fool out of yourself, Hansen... Playing well is cool, but, most importantly, just have fun... They can't hate on you if you play terrible but are still a decent guy.

First tee, first round. As a plus, we were able to survey the hole while driving in and also on our walk to the tee box to help us get off to a good start. We all talked about hitting irons to avoid a burn (a small channel of water) dissecting the first fairway. This was to be our warmup round, and what better way to start than *without* the driver going sideways into the burn, the road, or even worse, the clubhouse? Iron, it is.

I hadn't felt many nerves, which I found odd seeing as how these guys were mostly scratch golfers; and, to be clear, calling one a scratch golfer is a serious statement. As low as a two and high as a nine handicap over the past thirty years, I've been called a scratch by non-golfing friends who would brag about my abilities as if they knew. But let me assure you, I've never been a scratch or a zero like these guys.

Being a zero handicap means you shoot in the sixties some of the time and the low seventies most of the time. That is not me. That was, however, my new playing partners. They were true zeros. I currently carried the highest handicap of eight as I had been playing pretty poorly the past year while in and out of treatment, depression, and doctors' appointments. As I said before, it got ugly (for me at least – the highest it had been in ten years).

Being a slim six-foot-one with the build of a washed-up tennis player, I had decent form as a golfer. In fact, Alan would always introduce me with "This guy's got a greeeaat swing…" which essentially meant I could smooth it off the tee but couldn't chip and putt to save my life (or a par. Ha!). I would score in the low- to mid-seventies occasionally, but for the most part it was a seventy-five turned into an eighty-three with a few bladed and chunked chips throughout the round. The only scratch part of my game was me scratching my head after too many uncalled-for, double bogeys.

However, a couple of rounds (which I posted, Alan!) at my home course in the seventies and my play at Bushwood had me feeling good heading into this week. The overall game was back, and I had been working on the short game diligently for weeks. So, realizing my place in the world, we set off to task.

Time to swim with the sharks.

Roz led us off, with a swing I would say was akin to Tom Watson – a simple and quick turn of the body while bringing the club up and back down in perfectly mirrored fashion and tempo. Nothing to see here except a ball hit straight down the middle. The rest of our four- and five-irons penetrated the breeze and all found the fairway. It had begun and I didn't make a fool of myself. A sand wedge to the green left me with thirty feet to the hole. My putt went about twenty-seven feet. Uh oh… can't start with a bogey. "That's good, EH, pick it up," shouted Barney. And I did, as quickly as I could.

Because it was a warm-up round, putts were being graciously "given." In some stroke play (but mostly match-play situations), it's customary to give a putt to your opponent when you feel that they are going to make it. Or, it can be a sign of respect, a simple gesture to garner favor, or maybe to speed up play. Sometimes, putts are given just to avoid having to watch a friend or foe miss another one. In this case, they were just being plain nice which came as a welcome sign. It's hard to enjoy golf where you're just grinding to get it in the hole in a friendly game.

When the game of golf was in its youth, the standard distance for a putt given would be about twelve inches or "inside the leather." This can be confusing because back then when putters all had leather grips, they were all pretty much the same size. Back in the '80s and '90s, putters started taking on all kinds of weird shapes and lengths with rubber grips, making the "leather" part hard to discern. Nowadays the concept has changed and is widely accepted as the distance from the top of your putter head up the shaft to the bottom edge of your putter's grip – about twenty-four inches. To visualize this, most golfers will insert the head of the putter into the hole and then lay the putter down on the putting surface next to the ball. If the ball is between the hole and where the shaft ends and grip starts, it should be given. But it doesn't have to be. This gimmie measurement is also sometimes called the "Circle of Friendship," and today, for our first round, that distance increased somewhat dramatically to around three feet. With the help of this new friendship circle on the first couple of greens, I was at even par now through three holes and thinking maybe I could keep up with these guys.

Whoa, hold on...take it easy, Tiger, it's a long trip.

It was always fun getting to know new golfers and seeing new swings. Scott "Wilk" Wilkinson was one of those. A power player, Wilk was built like a mountain with the shoulders of a Mack truck coming up in your rearview mirror. During his swing, he would take his club up to the top and then, a pause, followed by hell-bent fury on the way back to the poor ball. If he connected well, he would hold his pose until it landed and rolled out a mile away. However, if he was the slightest bit off on contact, all the power would send the ball sideways followed by a self-chastising, "Piss off!!"

In stark contrast, Barney Barnett was about half his size at about a hundred and fifty pounds dripping wet, but with a swing so smooth and consistent it produced a perfect draw from left to right and on target nearly every time. Not only that, he out-drove us on most holes. Having competed at a

high level in college and worked for various club and ball man-
ufacturers (currently Bridgestone), he had honed his swing into
an effective mix of balance and effortless power.

It was somewhere in the middle of this opening round that I
would begin to identify the separation of talent between myself
and my newfound playing partners. After all, four of them
competed at "University" (look at me, talking like a Brit already). After the turn of the 9th hole, they were still driving the
ball straight and getting up and down when they missed an
approach. I, however, had been struggling with my short game
for some time and it showed. All the work and practice leading
up to this was not paying off.

The lies around the greens were very tight (meaning the grass
was very short) and chips needed to be clipped perfectly from
the turf. For me and my lack of confidence, pars were turned
into bogey and double bogeys quite easily, and not so much for
them. But one rule that was put in place to keep it fun was that
of "max double bogey" (where you would pick up if putting
for a double and only take a two-over score). I would come to
exercise it frequently -a little too frequently, in fact. Enter my
new pal, "Secret Agent-Max Double."

As we made our way around the course, there were quite a few
good par fours and man, these bunkers were deep. The par
threes were challenging as well, and I tried to consciously remember to play the Penfolds, but didn't do a great job. Not
because of the ball – heck, even though the ball was non-confirming to the PGA, Euro Tour, Liv, et cetera, it still had a
great feel to it, and I honestly didn't notice a difference between
it and my Titleist ProV1. The real problem was this: switching

out a ball during a round was not natural because it was usually illegal to do; unless it was damaged. As such, Wilk called me out on it on the 14th after I hit a nice 5 iron closest to the pin.

"Nice shot," he said, "but did you play the Penfold?"

"No…dammit!"

You see, Wilk is a lawyer from Denver, and it was clear that *nothing* escaped his attention, so I would have to improvise. On the last par three, when Wilk made an all-world par with his Penfold, it was decided that he would be the winner. So, we cracked open the little gold bar and everyone took a swig of the California whisky within. We then enjoyed hacking out the remainder of the holes into the breeze just a little bit more. In the end, this little gold trophy/keepsake had served its lame but fun purpose.

After finishing up the round we jumped aboard the shuttle with Neil and headed back to the Princes Lodge to check into our accommodations for the first two nights. We each had our own rooms, which was a nice start to the trip, and I was hoping it would help deal with any jetlag that might ensue from the nine-hour time change. A seven p.m. dinner was announced by text, so we met down at the bar around six for a couple of pints then sat down to our table to dine and talk about the first round.

The most important task of the evening was at hand: adding up the scores. With my course-adjusted handicap of ten, I would have ended up winning three skins, and, more importantly, canceling out some skins of others. This was met with a grumble from Alan right away and I found it hard to argue his point. I'm not a bad player but would agree that my ability to make pars on the ten toughest holes and negate some awesome natural birdies (without handicap strokes) wouldn't be fair. So, we all agreed anyone above zero or scratch would only get half their adjusted handicap number on skins since there was a decent amount of money on the line. Once adjusted, I ended up with one of the five or six skins of the group and took the team win with Wilk. Still a great first day.

Royal St. George's – Course 2, Day 2

Golf...Royal Golf...

The Royal St. George's Golf Club, located in Sandwich, Kent, England, is one of the courses on The Open Championship Rotation and the only Open Rota golf course to be located in South East England. It has hosted fifteen Open championships, the first in 1894 when it became the first club outside Scotland to host. Past champions include Collin Morikawa, Darren Clarke, Ben Curtis, Greg Norman, Sandy Lyle, Bill Rogers, Bobby Locke, Reg Whitcombe, Henry Cotton, Walter Hagen (on two occasions), Harry Vardon (on two occasions), Jack White and John Henry Taylor. It has also hosted The Amateur Championship on fourteen occasions.

The club was founded by the surgeon Laidlaw Purves in 1887 in the setting of wild duneland. Many holes feature blind or partially blind shots, although the unfairness element has been reduced somewhat after several twentieth-century modifications. The course also possesses the deepest bunker in championship golf, located on its fourth hole.[2]

***

The guys are talking this one up big. As in, this might be the best course we play on this trip. I guess I hadn't expected this. I always felt this would be more of a crescendo building up to the last day at Royal Liverpool or, as they call it, Hoylake. St. George's sat on the property adjacent to the Princes Lodge and golf course where we were staying; however, there was a bit of a roundabout way of getting there.

Neil helped us load into the shuttle and we headed back down the winding beachfront road towards Deal, until we made a right and started heading inland. About five houses in we passed an all-white house, with a plaque out front that read "The Whitehall." This was the former home of Ian Flemming, the writer and former naval intelligence commander who penned the original twelve James Bond novels, along with two collections of short stories about the world's most famous spy.

Turns out, Royal St. George's would be the inspiration behind the most famous golf match that never happened – *not* Cinque Ports, as I had thought. We had played my stupid little game on the wrong course! Oh well.

I said I was jetlagged, people.

---

[2] "Royal St. Georges Golf Club. January 3, 2023. In Wikipedia. https://en.wikipedia.org/wiki/Royal_St_George%27s_Golf_Club

In addition to his careers as a novelist and spy, Fleming (1908-64) was also a traveler, bon viveur, and sportsman – and he loved to escape to Kent to indulge his passions, including golf. After the War, he often motored down from London in his Ford Thunderbird on a Friday, in time for nine or eighteen holes before tea and, of course, a dry martini in the clubhouse – "shaken, not stirred."

It was here that he wrote "the spy story to end all spy stories" - and where he drew inspiration for all the Bond stories to come. Even the 007 tag came from the number of the London to Dover coach, now a National Express service.[3]

***

As a huge Bond fan, I was finding this really interesting. Dare I say, I was downright giddy!

We checked in at the St Georges pro shop and got some range balls to warm up. We were told the range was just down the way past the cart barn. Measuring about a quarter mile, it was not a short walk but at least our legs were warmed up when we got there.

Upon arrival, we noticed another group of Americans further down the range. We couldn't help but wonder about their playing abilities, but it looks like they're straight out of a J Crew catalog, with gelled-up hair and perfectly matching golf attire.

---

[3] "Explore James Bond's Kent". N.D. https://www.visitkent.co.uk/see-and-do/inspirational-ideas/explore-james-bonds-kent/#:~:text=After%20the%20war%2C%20he%20often,'Shaken%2C%20not%20stirred'.

A beautiful assortment of Yanks, for sure, and I was expecting a hard seltzer commercial to break out at any moment. I bet they smelled amazing. Could they play was the question.

That question was answered within ten seconds as one of the guys, on his attempted excavation of three inches of topsoil, caught the ropes set down to mark the hitting channel and almost clotheslined half the people on the range. He was now stuck in a spider web of braided nylon string as his friends tried to help him get free. We tried not to laugh as I'm sure that with a crew like ours we'd all embarrassed ourselves plenty at the range over the years. We finished hitting balls and, after a half-mile walk back in eighty-seven-degree weather, arrived back at the practice green adjacent to the first tee box. We were a Royal sweaty mess, but we were ready to tee off.

Way back in May, I had asked our tour service, Perry Golf, for a full caddie at all the Royal courses simply to enjoy the experience of walking the world's best links courses without towing a trolley (and maybe even to feel a little regal). A young New Zealander with an earring and square specs walked over, introduced himself as Kahoo, and announced he would be my looper. He wasn't exactly what I expected, but then again I've found that there seems to be no formula for a caddy and I've yet to see any two look the same.

We headed to the first tee, where random partners were drawn amongst our group, and Wilk and I were paired together as a "two-ball" (That's over- the-pond golf-speak for a twosome).

While I'd played golf courses that had a dedicated person as a starter before, St. George's was unique. There before us stood an elderly gentleman with a white, button-down short-sleeve shirt, oxford tie, pressed blue shorts, straw fedora with a red and blue band, and, of course, blue knee-high socks. He certainly looked the part, but it was the way he kept time that was most interesting. The starter hut from which he came resembled a small cottage with brown walls, white French doors and windows, and a thatch roof with a gold weathervane on it. We noticed it had "11:08" spelled out on individual boards (one square for each number) to denote the tee time. When our time came up, he walked over, took down the "0" and the "8," and replaced them with a "1" and "3" to reveal our tee time: 11:13.

How awesome. Who needs a Rolex anyway?

As we stood on the tee of our first ROTA course, ready to go, a small crowd gathered. Neil was taking videos; others were taking pics. Wilk hit a beauty down the left and I hit a good drive right down the middle; it looked perfect but then found the rough as it rolled out. Welcome to links golf.

No matter, because for my second shot, Kahoo gave me some advice on where to land the ball since it was a blind approach, and I hit a shot that landed a foot from the flag - a great start. I missed birdie on a bad read which turned it into a so-so start. When you hire a caddie, you really must accept the fact that they are not all perfect or even experts – Kahoo, for example, admittedly started caddying just four months earlier. But he's still got more loops than me, I'm sure.

I max-doubled the 2nd with a poor drive followed by a poor iron and four more poor attempts to hole my ball. The 3rd hole was a par three with a cool-looking chute that funneled you uphill into a three-tiered, blob-of-a-green the size of a Wal-mart. With large mounds surrounding it for protection, it was framed beautifully but looked like it could be truly penalizing. Wilk hit his 4-iron right, up and over said mounds and looked to fall victim to the design, only to make the recovery and par of a lifetime on a completely blind pitch shot! I reached out for a fist bump and noticed for the first time that his mitt was the size of a toaster. I had hit a decent iron to the front but still about forty yards away, I could only manage a three-putt bogey (one for each tier I had to putt over. Admittedly, I booed my-self a little here. Links greens can be massive and easy to hit, but that means nothing when you're still a mile from the hole.

Next up came the famed 4th hole... and, with it, the world's deepest bunker. It's basically a hillside moon crater about thirty feet high with A LOT of sand in it. Kahoo pointed out that if you managed to clear it, the hole would dogleg left toward Ian Fleming's Whitehall house. The goal from our forward tees, he explained, was to get it airborne with a 3-wood around two-hundred forty yards. If we could do that, this monster trap would not necessarily be in play. "People said this hole was hard," we said, but when Kahoo motioned with a finger back to the pro tees, we realized that we were getting a huge break. Looking back seventy yards, I couldn't even imagine trying to hit over, then probably into (and then out of) that hazard. It could take days to escape!

After Kahoo gave us his instructions, he ran ahead and stood atop the giant bunker to forecaddie and gave us a line to follow, since it was blocking our view of the fairway from the tee.

Wilk and I managed to hit identical shots just over and right of young Kahoo and, without a flinch, he followed our projectiles as they passed just over him with a hiss. He gave us both the safe signal and, as it turns out, our balls ended up about a foot from each other.

As we visualized our approach, I noticed this green resembled a huge potato chip with a giant bowl on the left that would probably funnel everything off the green if not hit on target. The pin was back right, and Kahoo advised us to use Fleming's Whitehall chimney off in the distance as a target to avoid the valley of Frito Lay. I swear I was listening to Kahoo – but my ball must not have been, which just after impact curled and landed left of the green. Wilk proceeded to push his shot right.

As we walked up to the putting surface, I found my ball sitting down in the bowl (I was supposed to avoid) and I was pringled, essentially. Unfortunately, the hole was now some sixty feet away, eight feet up above me, and just ten feet from the back of the green. Another green hit, but another impossible putt. Welcome again to Links Golf.

Thinking of the consequences of a bad stroke, anything short would roll back to me, and anything long would head off the back like a locomotive and possibly into Ian's petunias. I locked out the doubt, shut off the brain, and just whacked one on Kahoo's line, managing to snug it up there to two feet … just inside the friendship circle. Conceded par seemed a victory. I think Ian would be proud. Bond would too. Goldfinger… not so much.

Wilk and I continued to play the front nine in good form, making some decent irons shots but almost all coming from out of the rough. One thing I learned very quickly that was no matter how many times a caddie or a playing partner said, "Good Drive!" or "Right down the middle!" you were not guaranteed a coveted position in these fairways. So many bumps and humps on this sun-baked turf meant your "drilled," "piped," or "crushed" drive was just as likely to find the fescue or bunker than the fairway it set out for.

As hot as it was, the bottles of water supplied by Kahoo on the 1st tee were running dry and it was a relief to see a drinking fountain in between the 7th and 8th holes. As Kahoo approached, I wasn't paying attention to the fact that he had turned the secondary lower faucet on that was meant for a watering hose. As he began to drink from the top dispenser, I walked up and began to wait. As I waited, I noticed this lower faucet running and, in my California draught avoidance mode, turned it off. As I did, the pressure built back up and shot out of the top, completely soaking poor Kahoo.

Oh, so that's why that was on...I see now.

We laughed as I apologized for being so dense. As I handed him my towel, he said he didn't mind the shower much...it was damn hot for England.

Overall, Royal St. George was a fantastic romp of a course. The bunkers were the stars of the production and I swear some of these traps had teeth around them. I was lucky enough to find only a six or seven and when I did, the sand was so consistent I managed to hit the best bunker shots in a long time; snuggling up for tap-ins or conceded pars. On some, I felt lucky just to get out alive.

We finished up and headed to the pro shop to empty our pockets on St. George's collectible course flags and ball markers and then over to the patio for a quick Bulmers Cider to add up the scores. As Murph tallied up the numbers, he casually mentioned "Hmmm, yup…uh huh…Alan shot sixty-seven."

Two or three of us replied with, "Wait, what?"

"Yeah, sixty-seven…and it was a pleasure to watch."

Sadly, I think he only won a mere two skins but clearly deserved more than that. I think JoeBro and I canceled a couple of his birdies with mediocre pars with a stroke. We just couldn't figure it. With an eighty-four I managed one skin and felt incredibly fortunate, but Alan would suffer on the payouts despite his brilliant round…and he had recommended the game setup. He could see him rethinking it, so I tried cheering him up with "Hey, the money will come and go but a 67 at Royal St. George? Give me that any day! He conceded the point with a half-smile and we packed up and hopped on the bus.

I can't remember, but at some point between the previous night's dinner and drinks and the shuttle over, Barney had shouted out, "Hey, we gotta jump in the English Channel when we get done playin'! I mean, we're here, right? Wouldn't that be great??"

Now, had this been typical England weather in the sixties, we would have scoffed at such a proposition. However, at eighty-seven degrees – and with a few ciders down our gullets – it wasn't long before there were four or five takers on the ride back to the lodge. I hadn't yet committed, thinking the channel had to be so cold it would turn my hard-earned Florida tan bright white on pure shock alone (or worse, turn my unmentionable into a stack of dimes). But seeing the locals out enjoying the beach on the way back made it seem much more feasible. So, I headed to the room, stripped off the undies, threw the golf shorts back on having forgotten to bring a suit, and headed down to the front entrance. (In hindsight, I should have rinsed those shorts out much better before the long trip north because OH MAN, did they reek!)

Once out front, I found Dobler, Barney, and JoeBro with towels in hand and ready for the sand. Our trusty ward Neil also had his phone out ready to take some pics. While waiting for any more takers Neil and I began talking. At around sixty, Neil is happily married and has three girls and a granddaughter. He's been in hospitality most of his life with a brief stint in healthcare before becoming a driver. So, it made sense that not only did he drive us around with great hospitality but also helped document with plenty of pics.

We had to wear footwear to get down to the water as the rocks, although rounded and smooth, were tough to navigate for our white, pillowy, golfer's feet. Once over the rocks, I entered the water and waited for the shock to hit me at about sixty-two degrees like back on our Pacific beaches, but it didn't. In fact, it felt like seventy-five. It couldn't be! But it was. Once the water got past the mid-section with the help of a few waves, it was bliss. Yes, there we were, in the English Channel, swimming around...like fish...and some small waves...and oh hey, there's a seal...

Wait, What the - ???

Not more than twenty feet to our one o'clock we saw a seal pop its head out to take a look at us. "Hey was that, Murph?" someone shouted out. We laughed. This was fun. "Great idea, Barney!" As we finished up our swim and exited the water, Neil snapped a pic to commemorate the moment and we walked back across the street to the Lodge.

That night we had a great dinner in the bar and many more dark fruit ciders. Soon we were out on the patio watching the sun go down over the sixth green on the Prince's Shores course. Like an orange egg yolk, it began to settle down into its green albumen, which was pierced by a toothpick with a flag on it.

Just adjacent to the lodge and its patio, was a huge practice green. Even though this wasn't a clubhouse or pro shop connected to a course, Prince's Lodge, in a brilliant move, had built this green as a place for the golfer alum groups like us to imbibe with a few pints and roll a few putts… and maybe even play some games.

As the sun passed the horizon, Barney said with utmost enthusiasm, "Alright guys, we're going to play a game called "Balls Deep."

Now before your mind starts running wild, this is simply a basketball-like free-throw of your golf ball onto the putting green to a designated hole. At only five quid buy-in per round, this would not only be a fun little game but would unfold into a controversy for the ages known as "Operation Euro-Wash."

Before I left for the UK, my wife had discovered some euros from our last trip abroad. It was a hundred euros in ten-pound notes, to be exact. I'm in Europe about once a decade and, having forgotten about that little thing called Brexit, I just assumed that euros were still good in the UK.

As we played our game, we had all come close to making a couple by lofting our balls onto the green, guessing the slope and runout, and once in a while, hitting the pin. But no wins for a while. This was harder than we thought! Finally, Dobler canned one and we all cheered. It was time to pay up, so I simply handed him a 10 note and asked for a five back. He complied.

It was getting dark now, and it only made the rounds more intense. Barney decided to double the buy-in. Ten minutes had gone by with some misses and retrievals of the balls back to their owners, so Wilk took a break from the game by ordering, and eating, not one, but three sticky toffee puddings. Now, with a full-on sugar rush, he rejoined, and proceeded to hole a bomb from long range.

"Here's a ten, buddy," I said.

Great. Next winner...Al. "Here's a ten, Al!"

"Okay," he complied.

After a half-dozen rounds of Balls Deep, I had inadvertently managed to get all my euros out into circulation.

Princes –
Course 3, Day 3

The Yanks Take Over the Back 9

Prince's Golf Club was financed by Sir Harry Mallaby-Deeley, Bt, and designed by Charles Hutchings, the 1902 Amateur Champion, on land donated by the Earl of Guilford. It was completed late in 1906 as an eighteen-hole course and was the first course designed to counter the effects and distances of the significantly longer Haskell ball. Club captain A.J. Balfour, a former British Prime Minister, drove the first ball in the Founder's Vase in June 1907.

The present-day twenty-seven-hole layout is the result of a 1950 redesign following wartime damage to the original course. World War II was very hard on Prince's, but Australian entrepreneur Sir Aynsley Bridgland intervened, engaging Sir Guy Campbell and John Morrison to redesign and restore the course.

The late WWII ace, Member of Parliament, and 1949 Walker

Cup captain Percy Belgrave "Laddie" Lucas was born in the old clubhouse at Prince's, his father being the first club secretary. During WWII, Lucas used his knowledge of the course to make an emergency landing after his Spitfire was crippled over northern France. Today, a commemorative plaque by the 4th tee on the Himalayas course marks the spot where he landed. In memory of Lucas, Prince's hosts an annual golf tournament, the Laddie Lucas Spoon, for boys and girls aged eight to thirteen.[4]

***

The English love their eggs and the breakfast menu at the Lodge had eight wonderful variations from which to choose. I picked the Scottish breakfast with smoked salmon, and it was perfectly done - a great way to start. After we finished up, I brought my suitcase and clubs down to the shuttle as we'd be heading up to Wales straight from the course right after the round.

The Prince's Golf Club was about a mile down the road from the Lodge and included three nines - The Himalayas, The Shores, and The Dunes. We were set to play the Himalayas and the Shores. Our earliest tee time so far, we found the range at seven a.m. after walking through a grouping of gorgeous tall pine trees guiding us to the practice facility. As we warmed up and hit balls into the distance, it was hard not to notice the giant factory about two miles away. Alan mentioned it was

---

4 "Prince's Golf Club, Sandwich. February 4, 2023. In Wikipedia. https://en.wikipedia.org/wiki/Prince%27s_Golf_Club,_Sandwich#:~:text=Prince's%20was%20financed%20by%20Sir,the%20significantly%20longer%20Haskell%20ball.

Pfizer's…and their largest Viagra plant, so I shot out a quick, obligatory joke. "I heard it was about half that size until they had a major spill and grew twice as large for about two hours…then doctors were called." Even though it was a dad joke I got a few laughs. The foursomes for the day were Alan, Barney, Roz, and me followed by Murph, Wilk, JoeBro, and Dobler.

For me, there is nothing like golf on a clear, cool, sunny morning. The shadows run deep into the course and not only help with perspective but give detail to the shapely undulations in the fairways and greens that would otherwise go unnoticed with overhead sun or gray. Even more, the dew on the grass unveils the footprints and trolley tracks of the few explorers of the game before us as well as their putting lines, which might help to show us the way "home.'

The first hole on the Himalayas had lined forest walls to each side to start out, which framed them like a picture as we hit out to a wide-open landing area. High tall grasses came out from the trees as a third cut of rough and guarded against any corner cutting you might have considered from the tee box.

However, the fescued rough here in the coastal South of England was fairly sparse in most areas so it wasn't too difficult to find the ball. When you did, it was pretty easy to get a club on it – unless, of course, you got into some perilously deep stuff or a gorse bush. Ergo, if you could find it you almost always had a shot. The only problem is that it comes out hot, with absolutely no spin. And with these elevated, domed greens, it wouldn't hold for very long without running off in one direction or the other. This I would learn time and time again with Secret Agent Max Double as my witness.

The Himalayas nine was a fairly tame test of golf with most of the holes running back and forth alongside each other. They were, however, uniquely dotted with points of interest. After the third hole, just behind the green, stood the propeller monument and a plaque denoting the area where Percy had landed his spitfire. Barney took time to read the details and summarize for us on the fourth tee box. Holes 4-7 were fairly uneventful but then we came to a short, three-hundred and twenty-yard par four as the 8th. The elevated tee box was just a bit right of the fairway, but from then on down the fairway it resembled a bowling alley: totally straight with little rough and bunkers down the sides but walled off with tall weeds on both sides.

"Looks drivable from here, fellas, what do you recommend?" asked Dobler. Without thinking, I blurted out a line from a favorite movie of mine:

"I recommend you stop acting like such a ..."

I'll let you imagine the rest. They knew the movie and this caught everyone off-guard; and Barney, who was trying to hit his tee ball, had to pull off his shot as we all hit the ground laughing. Timing is everything.

We were still licking our chops at the thought of driving the green as barney hit a nice drive down the right. Alan went next, and with the low, punchy, trap-draw he was known for, landed it just on the front edge. For those not familiar with a "punchy trap-draw," it's one of the coolest shots in golf. Essentially, this inside-to-outside swing comes down fairly steep and on top of the ball, slightly "trapping" it between the club head and the ground. This causes it to kind of "squirt out" under pressure. The resulting shot is a ball that comes out with a low, hissing sound from the spin applied from said pressure with a right-to-left curve of about five to ten yards in perfect control. Alan has perfected it, and I enjoy watching it every time.

"Great shot, Al!" we all said as I stepped up. I had decided on my typical shot, which is the exact opposite of Alan's: a high fade from left to right aimed just left of the hole for compensation. I gave a good strike right on my intended line, then we all watched it carry high down the left… and it kept on going. A couple of rare, straightforward bounces would do the trick and put me on the putting surface just twenty-five feet left of the pin for eagle. Roz and Barney were just short and would chip up for birdie chances. I hadn't had a birdie yet, but this situation looked promising. My putt had a left-to-right line and with firm intentions as I hit it, found its way to the hole. Eagle! Would I win a skin? Only time would tell, but with the talented foursome of golfers I knew behind us nothing was guaranteed.

Links courses can be a major challenge without knowing where to hit your shot; this is what makes caddies so important. However, without one today, Roz's journey on the 9th hole would be one we'll never forget. We both hit drives that looked good off the tee, but found the left fairway bunker; only he had rolled up against the bottom of a serious wall on the front left. This meant his only option was to come out sideways. The only problem was it had to be to the right toward the fairway in my direction with no right-handed stance. So, he took a left-handed grip with his iron, swung lefty a la Phil Mickelson, and hit it with the back of the club out sideways, just narrowly getting it out of the bunker on the right side. It almost curled back in, but I was impressed. Now, while having to stand in the bunker, with the ball above his feet, he would unwillingly draw his next shot left into a more famous bunker on the front left of the green – the Sarazen bunker.

Little did we know that this particular bunker had played a major part in golf history. Turned out (as we learned upon reading the plaque nailed to the side), it was played by American Gene Sarazen on his way to a five-shot victory over fellow yank Macdonald Smith nearly eighty years ago. Best of all, it was done with a club that Sarazen had designed for this very event: one with a fat, smooth bottom, and an added pronounced flange so the club would not dig into the sand like all the others did. Instead, this flange would glide or kind of bounce off the bottom of the hazard as the sand compressed, helping the ball pop out on its own pillow of sand. From that day on, the Gene Sarazen Sand Iron (known to us as the "Sand Wedge") was born. This miraculous invention was put to market quickly after his victory as the R-90 and became one of Wilson's best-selling golf clubs of all time.

Nostalgia aside, this bunker Roz was in was also a bit scary. It had a giant six- or seven-foot wall blocking any view of the green like so many others here in the UK, but this wall had railroad ties embedded vertically into the face. It almost appeared as though they were holding up the massive lip of the bunker, like a scaffolding that was topped with tall fescue. If one should happen to "blade" or catch one "thin" out of this hazard, there was a good chance it would rebound and come back at you faster than you could react.

With Roz's skillset and most modern sand wedge, he would get his ball up and over the lip and up and down with two putts for what we could call "a pretty damn good bogey!"

As we made the turn for the Shores' nine we were reminded of the importance of having a starter on the first tee boxes for courses with three nines. It can be a source of confusion and often requires a level of traffic control by the course. Our group teed off all fine and well for the 10th and had started walking down the mowed path to the fairway when we saw a group of golf carts (they call them "buggies" across the pond – adorable) pull up to the tee and start lining up to start their round. Not a minute later our group came up expecting to have the right of way to continue the round. They were up there for so long we were wondering if there was any issue. Turns out there was. From what Wilk told us, words were exchanged, and the buggy boys let our guys through to stay behind us; however, it wasn't without some harsh attitude and commentary, including, "Fookin' Americans!"

As the round progressed, it was obvious who the real "fookers" were as we watched them drive their buggies all over the course and up alongside the greens while falling well behind.

The Shores course was decent enough as it started down alongside the oceanside road Neil had brought us in on. We had to pause on a few shots as beach-going folks crossed through the fairways riding bikes and walking dogs, which really added to the overall accessible feeling of this course here on the Sandwich coast. As we came up to the 12th , we felt as though we were right back where we started the morning at the Prince's Lodge, which was a welcome sight. It was eighty-five degrees, we were dying of thirst, and the water from the fountains here seemed to make us more so. We stopped in for some water and biscuits to hold off our hunger until we could make it back to the clubhouse.

The first six or seven holes of the Shores were relatively easy and fun, but things got more serious coming down the stretch. In particular, the 17th was a long-haul par 5 that I chose to make significantly longer. Hitting it right off the tee, I found the deep stuff on a dinosaur-backed hump with seriously tall grass. Had it not been for my volunteer search party, I wouldn't have found it. Roz had the eyes of a hawk for finding balls, but I kind of wish we'd had let this one stay lost. Another miss down the right from this ugly lie found me in the same situation, only a hundred yards further. I could tell fatigue was setting in from working in and out of the stuff all day with my trolley in tow as I must have dumped my bag over six or seven times.

I wasn't thinking straight either. As a result, my next shot was just as poor as I hacked out a 4 iron even further right into a vast area of sand the size of the Sahara. What was I doing? Now that I think about it, I should have played out sideways…at least twice on this hole already! As I walked through this expanse of desert surrounded by gorse, fescue, and bramble berry bushes, I began to lose sight of my party.

Uh oh. Maybe they should send a plane out to look for me.

Then I came upon something peculiar; and a bit unnerving…bones. Calling on my days of studying anatomy in college, I identified one as a snapped femur. The bones looked a bit big for a human, but I was unsure.

These are animal bones, right? Or have there been others before me that never made it out?

With no luck in finding my ball, I dropped one mostly for fun and hit it with agent Max Double waiting for me up on the green. Double was my destiny, but, as it turned out, not the last. Double on 18 from a terrible bounce would further disgust my finish. Oh well, I just thought about the eagle on the front nine as my one moment to remember and hoped to get a skin.

After a quick shower in the clubhouse to wash off the last eighteen holes and a pound of sand, we grabbed lunch and counted the scores before the long ride to Bridgend, in the South of Wales. It's an eighty-three for me and I felt lucky again to get a team win with blind partner Wilk while also nabbing a skin for the eagle. Job done to wrap up our time in Sandwich. And if you think I like talking about the town Sandwich because I just like saying it, you're right - Sandwich!

"Lechyd da!"

The ride west to Wales was a long one – over seven hours with traffic and bio breaks. As we got out of the van at a rest stop called the Road Chef, we noticed it was about ninety-five degrees. Needing ice for our pints and ciders, we were turned away at every store…sometimes with a laugh. It was just overwhelming for the UK to be this hot for so long. Dejected and back on the bus, we now headed into Dobler's territory, Wales. He told us that tradition must prevail, and we needed to take a shot when we headed over the Prince of Wales Bridge. We all poured a shot of Jameson in a cheap paper cup and prepared to comply as the middle of the bridge drew near.

"Lechyd da!" they all shouted.

This was a new one to me, but Dobler explained it means "To your health!" in Welsh. I responded with a shout for another shot so I could join in. "Lechyd da!" It was in moments like this that I felt even more like part of the group.

As we rolled close to Bridgend, we saw a couple of interesting businesses such as "Rambos Off License," which was appar-

ently a betting parlor; "Butty Licious" for Butties (or sand-
wiches, as they call them); and "Peaky Barbers" (no doubt de-
rived from the Netflix sensation *Peaky Blinders*). Should we
stop? A lot could be accomplished here within an hour - some
of it fun and some of it...well...could be trouble.

Now fully into our destination town of Laleston, we rolled up
to our shelter for the next two nights called the Great House.
On the itinerary, it's labeled as the most "rustic" and "cozy" of
the lodgings (in marketing speak, this apparently means old
and small). As we were unpacking the bus, we noticed both a
catering van and DJ van parked in the lot. After seeing a lot of
people sweating their arses off in tuxedos and gowns, it became
obvious that there was a wedding happening that evening on
the smallish property, and we were not expecting that.

It was still sweltering out, so, hoping to go to cool off in our
rooms before dinner, we stepped up to what looked to be a tiny
pub/desk/sitting room/lobby to get our room keys. Turned
out, these hotel rooms had no cooling and the Great House
had become a stone dungeon-turned-sauna – at another twenty
degrees warmer than outside. Barney just laughed and shook
his head. "This is great... we're going to remember this for a
long time." No kidding, Barney. I looked at Alan (my new
roommate), who at six foot-six didn't look like he'd fit inside
the room, let alone on any furniture within. I'm shaking my
head too and laughing in disbelief.

Our room was upstairs and right over the reception desk,
which was fine enough, but our windows faced the small parking lot which many weddinggoers had already filled up. It also

faced the setting sun to ensure maximum temps before bed-time. Gasping for a cross breeze of any kind, I went down to the front desk to ask for a fan and was told they are fresh out. Later at dinner, Wilk informed me he got there right before me to get the last one.

You son of a…

I'm kidding. I had to respect Wilk's hustle as both decisive and speedy (especially for a man of his size trying to negotiate this tiny stone labyrinth). As for me and Alan, we would have to keep our one window open all night hoping it would cool down. The only problem was our one window faced the only open window for the wedding reception area…where the DJ was set up. From the look of it, that small semi-subterranean dungeon was going to be the hottest dance party in town… literally.

I opened up my suitcase and sensed a slight odor immediately. Remember those shorts I used to swim in the English Channel? Although I had diligently washed them in the shower and hung them up to dry, they were still a bit damp when I wrapped them in their own plastic bag. Thank God I did at least that much, because when I opened that bag the smell was unreal. I had to apologize immediately to Alan within our first few minutes of rooming together. "Sorry buddy, I brought the English Channel with me!"

To get it out of our heads, we headed out to dinner across the street at a pub/restaurant next door called El Prado. The idea was to drink enough beer to cripple an ox, thinking it would help us crash hard and cope with the smell, heat, and wedding noise we would encounter when we got back. Maybe the party might even be over when we returned?

No such luck.

We got back to find it still going strong, with many of the guests out in the courtyard and parking lot mixing it up. Around eleven p.m. we turned in and did our best to enjoy the wedding reception music, which was a random, trance-style mix of Elton John and Cher.

Typical of trance music, the chorus repeated about fifty-seven times. Maybe fifty-eight. In my delirium I lost count, even though I had earplugs in. Let's put it this way: that night, and for much of the next day, I too was questioning whether I believe in life after love.

I was heated, but felt more sympathy for Alan while he tried to balance and sleep on a bed the width of a handrail. His golf bag may have been more comfortable (but at least the room was "cozy"). We managed a few hours of sleep as it cooled off somewhere between three and seven a.m.

The morning came too soon in this once again peaceful little town, and we had breakfast down in the dungeon where the reception had taken place just hours earlier. We swapped stories of sleep deprivation, and Roz shared with us his newfound favorite TV show, *Goggle Box*. This is a TV show about people watching a bunch of TV shows while they add commentary.

In this particular episode, the "Goggleboxers" were watching a show called *Naked Attraction*. From Roz's description it sounded like *The Dating Game,* however, in this version, they reveal the entire body of a person slowly, working from bottom to top, while adding commentary until they were completely naked. Roz then fed us the commentary from both the Goggleboxers (an older man and his wife) with a slight accent. "Wot…is he signaling for a left tuuurrrn?" or "Needs a bit a gardening, don't ya think, Mum?" and the best: "Imagine ya pan the camera up from the feet and next are the t*%ts??!!..before the knees? Not good, Luv." You get the picture.

Once the contestant picked (a now-fully naked) one, two or three, the contestant then had to get undressed and come back out for all to see. Then the two would go on a date (with clothes on, of course).

At the end of the show, they visited former contestants and it sounded like none of these naked attractions were working at all, with most dates lasting minutes, at best!

Now, as intellectuals with a hangover, we discussed hypotheses such as, "Maybe the point here is that by showing how little the human body actually affects the relationship (when in fact you're only naked ten to twenty minutes out of the day) all that's left is putting up with each other's personalities and finding a common bond? Could this really be a brilliant sociological experiment that speaks to the shallowness of our ability to pick an actual companion…despite their looks?" Dobler replied in his Bostonian-Welsh accent, "You know that's a brilliant observation, but you're probably overthinking it." Could it be then that the show had nothing to do with trying to find mates and simply made jokes about the human body and got naked airtime for shock value?

Nah.

These Brits probably think they've come so far since the days of Benny Hill. They haven't...but still... it makes for some great television.

We ended our meal and table talk, whereby the entire breakfast club swore they'd be on the lookout for *Gogglebox* (and more specifically *Naked Attraction*) on the hotel telly going forward.

With some time to spare before the shuttle to Porthcawl, we decided to take a stroll through town and came across an incredible church just across the street. It was gated shut so the guys stayed out. As they wandered off, I saw that there was a service going on later in the day, so I decided to open the gate and enter St David's Church of Laleston for a look around.

***

In 1180, William, Earl of Gloucester, granted land in the area to William Lageles, from whom the village is thought to have gotten its name. The nave and chancel are believed to date to the late thirteenth and fourteenth centuries, and the southern porch and tower to the later medieval period. The tower interior is in the Perpendicular Gothic style. The church underwent restoration by John Prichard in 1871, and the stained-glass windows, probably by Clayton and Bell, are from that decade.[5]

---

[5] "St. David's Church, Laleston." April 6, 2023. In Wikipedia. https://en.wikipedia.org/wiki/St_David%27s_Church,_Laleston

I walked around to take photos and like so many churches of the era, it's surrounded by a cemetery. The land has moved and settled so much over the years that many of the headstones and above-ground monuments to the deceased had shifted and were angled all over the place. It's as if the dead were rising in one moment and time just stopped. Incredibly eerie. Or maybe this heat just got to them. I could relate.

As we packed up back at the Great House, I mentioned to Alan that I wanted to snap a few pics of him trying to get through the doorways and down the stairs because, well, it was just too funny. The pictures of Alan Stearns, lurking about the inn, his head obscured by the tops of most doorways, might just be the most popular of the trip. It's clear that whoever built this place could not have been over five-foot-five.

In conclusion, Barney was right. We'll have a hard time remembering the details of our other accommodations, but this one night, spent at the Great House, will live in our minds forever.

Royal Porthcawl – Course 4, Day 4

A Royal Beating

Royal Porthcawl Golf Club is a golf club in Wales in the United Kingdom, located north of Porthcawl and bordering the Bristol Channel. The club was founded in 1891 by a group of businessmen from Cardiff, with the first nine-hole golf course being laid out on Lock's Common by Charles Gibson the following year. In 1895, the club moved to its present location with the addition of a further nine-hole course. Shortly after that, the new course was extended to eighteen holes, with the original course later being abandoned. Royal status was conferred on the club by King Edward VII in 1909.[6]

***

A decent thirty-minute ride North and back over the bridge

---

[6] "Royal Porthcawl Golf Club." April 2,2023. In Wikipedia. https://en.wikipedia.org/wiki/Royal_Porthcawl_Golf_Club

(Lechyd-da!) got us out to the coast of Porthcawl Bay. At ten a.m. it was already eighty degrees and the beaches along the bay were jampacked. The Porthcawl Clubhouse sat above the cliffs looking down on the bay where, even though the tide was well out, the water was overloaded with paddleboarders and bathers looking for relief.

We checked into the pro shop and grabbed some balls for the range. Again, in what seems like a theme with these royal courses, the range is like a mile or two away (especially when it's uphill like this one was), hell and gone from the clubhouse. However, the road to get there runs next to the 18th hole, and as we walked alongside the fairway, I took time to scope out the finishing hole. Its layout had trouble left, right, and middle off the tee, and I was hoping the research would help in case we needed to make a par at the finish.

After hitting balls and working on the short game, we checked back into the pro shop. I asked the shopgirl about my caddie and she bragged that he was excellent as well as a plus-one handicap, so things were looking up. I had yet to have a caddie that was also a good golfer, so hopefully he was just the guy to get me around in under eighty strokes. His name was Lewis Mainwaring - *how English,* I thought. A young guy around twenty-three, he'd just come in from playing the course that morning. Introductions finished up and we headed out to the first tee to get tactical about our round together.

Today's group would be Dobler, Roz, Murph and me leading off, with Alan, Barney, JoeBro, and Wilk in tow. This was my first round with Murph, and I was looking forward to playing with a doctor who took up the game not long after med school but had managed to become really good in a short amount of time. It was apparent from witnessing him warm up on the range that he was athletic yet had probably manufactured his swing by himself.

What was most noticeable about it was his tempo – one that was so incredibly slow Barney would later describe it as "partially narcoleptic," even saying he thought Murph might have fallen asleep at the top of his swing at least a few times in the past. In fact, on one of the bus rides, Barney did a reenactment of Murph's swing, and, as he took it to the top, pretended to start snoring. It brought some of us to tears laughing.

But to draw a full picture of his "move," Murph would start his swing by slowly stretching the club straight back, making his entire hip and shoulder turn at the very top with a coiling maneuver. Then came a short pause for a second, followed by an underwhelming effort straight through the ball with hardly any legs on the follow-through. It was a swing that looked to be a slow-motion replay full of big arcs and stiff-looking triangles, but the results spoke for themselves. He hit it long and straight consistently and the tempo was a big part of it. Alan said on the tee box that anyone playing with him would have improved their tempo ten-fold by the end of the round just by watching him. There's a saying in golf that goes, "There are no pictures on the scorecard," meaning that no matter how you look swinging the club or get the ball in the hole, it's the score that matters. His swing didn't look bad or awkward by any measure, but was a picture of tempo, for sure.

I took note of the scorecard before folding and putting it in my pocket. On the front was a picture of the first tee of Porthcawl, and it appeared to be taken right from where we were standing. It was more breathtaking in real life, leading us downhill and then back up to an elevated green, with an amazing view of the ocean all down the left.

And we felt ready for every bit of it.

Lewis and I conferred on the first tee and he advised that 3 wood was the best club to avoid the bunkers at two-hundred-fifty yards down the hill. I watched my fellow players all hit their driver and go left, into the bunker, and right, into the other bunker. I took Lewis' advice and hit my 3 wood just short of the left bunker like we talked about. Well done, caddie, well done. Lewis and I settled into designing an approach up the hill, over a bunker to a back pin location, ninety-five yards away. He said, "Okay, I want you to hit this one ninety yards, ten feet right of the pin."

"Okay, sure," I replied.

I nodded and concurred and launched my ball with a fifty-four-degree wedge on his line to absolute perfection...to about three feet left of the hole. I made it for birdie. Lewis is the best caddie I've ever had. Not to ruin the suspense, but this would be my lone birdie of the day on my way to a disappointing score. To make matters worse, Alan also birdied it to cover me up on the skin!

Lewis continued to guide me well despite my errant shot-making, even giving me some short-game tips to help take the sting out of it and keep Max Double at bay.

When I asked him what he did outside of golf, he talked about becoming a dentist. A noble profession, and from his descriptions, it sounded like the dental game in the UK is more akin to the mafia as it's run under a triad of men who won't be relinquishing power any time soon. For now, he'd pay for his schooling while caddying, playing, and running the pro shop. He seemed to be a fine lad with a focused future.

The landscape of Porthcawl was amazing, with lots of elevation changes from tee to green and all the bunkers being well laid out (according to my ball which would find as many as possible). Lewis kindly mentioned that the breaks I had been getting were just brutal, with shot after shot finding the wrong bounce, or a false front, or hidden bunker. From his perspective, it seemed like I was the guy the architects were thinking of when they laid out the penalty areas. I would agree.

Dobler and Roz were playing well and all I could think of was that one of these poor guys might end up being my blind draw partner; so, unless I gained some focus coming in, I'd be doing them a disservice. Despite my poor play, Lewis commented, "This is honestly the best group of players I've ever caddied for." I knew he was serious, but when someone compliments your ability or points out how well you're playing, your game usually goes right into the tank. It's like a jinx. Turned out it was a bit too late for my round after taking max double on thirteen, fourteen, and sixteen, so while it didn't matter for me, I told him not to tell my partners until after the round.

I stepped up to 18 exhausted from four straight rounds (a first for me as I've never played more than three). To add insult to injury, I forgot the tee box was slotted all the way back toward the range, so we had to walk up and back and cross the road that led to the driving range we had walked earlier. An interesting choice by the designer, but upon turning around to face the hole I now saw why he did it. I was taken aback by how the hole itself was jaw-droppingly gorgeous as it flowed back to the clubhouse downhill and straight into the ocean while somehow crossing underneath the No. 1 tee complex.

Again, with a little focus, maybe it was not too late to help out my unknown partner in the blind draw or even grab a skin. "Come on, Erik, I know it hasn't been the best day, but you can still finish well, yeah?" Lewis said. I gave him a nod. I hit one of my better drives with a slight draw straight down the right side just short of the traps. Job done. Next, tempo-and-target swing thoughts launched a 7 iron down the hill a little left and onto the green. We both seriously misread the birdie putt and settled for a two-putt par. It's always great to end on a high note. I still really enjoyed the course regardless of the ninety I shot and, as it turns out, Dobler and I took second in the blind draw by a shot. You just never know.

We finished up our Porthcawl golf experience by drinking a few pints with some of the locals and enjoying the clubhouse, all the while overlooking the bay filled with the thousands of beachgoers enjoying their last weekend of summer. Upon exiting the pub, I ran into Lewy one last time, and we vowed to stay in touch and wish each other well as the group boarded the shuttle for our trip north.

Pen-Y-Fan, Brecons Beacons – Day 5 (The Supposed "Day Off")

An Upward Battle...For Some

Three weeks before the trip started, Alan was suffering from major back problems and could barely walk. We talked about rehabilitation and modalities almost daily. I knew he would get it figured out as we talked about doing yoga, working out, stretching, heating, icing, et cetera. It was an all-out war on back pain, and I'd been there many times.

Right before we were due to leave, I phoned him up.

"Hey man," I said, "nine days of golf is a major stretch...I've been researching all the courses and it looks like Pyle and Kenfig might be the ranked the lowest in the bunch. The idea of playing our fifth(!) eighteen in a row in the morning and then getting on a bus for four hours might be a little tough on the back."

He agreed and said he'd do some research on it and get back to me.

Within a few days of our conversation our local expert Dobler would agree with this, so we canceled P&K (the nickname for it) and decided for a day off to recover. Dobler, however, was coming up with some other plans.

About halfway to Southport where the second half of our trip would take place, was a mountainous reserve called Pen-y-fan. He explained to us that there was a great hike at Pen-Y-Fan, called Brecons Beacons, named for two large peaks at the end of a two-mile, forty-five-minute, "gradually uphill" trail. He told us, "Yeah, my daughter did it and it was easy for her, so you guys can do it with no problem!"

Now, I don't know about the others, but I hadn't walked eighteen holes in a long time, let alone seventy-two in four days. Like I said, I'm a lazy American who plays golf while riding in a cart while having a few beers. But in preparation for the trip, I'd been walking a few miles in the mornings to get ready. However, what I was finding is that the one thing you don't predict or expect is for your feet to be aching due to all the humps and bumps around links golf courses. It may look flat from the road but once you get out there, you can't find a flat surface until you reach the greens (i.e., my dogs were barkin' by day two!)

With that in mind, there we were, on our day off getting talked into, of all things, a hike... that went straight up a mountain.

But Dobler's daughter had done it....

It was a cloudy day and we were looking at rain at some point, so we brought our jackets (but little else) for protection. The trail seemed to be very popular as parking was scarce for a week-day. As we hit the main entrance there was a gate that took us over a river and onto the trailhead. There we noticed a lot of construction going on to turn this hike into an even bigger attraction. As we started up, there were tons of hikers with families and dogs going up or coming down, some of which had decided to tackle it with kids in a stroller (which seemed excessive given the large gaps in terrain we came upon).

The fitter portion of our small group attacked it aggressively and started to pass others on the way up just out for a stroll.

The not-so-fit, well not so much. About a quarter of the way up, they decided to turn back and help Neil "guard" the ice chest still on the bus.

I think they made the right choice, though, as our prize for hustling up the mountain was rain and wind at the perfect time to get soaked and then blown dry as we crested one of the beacons. It also turned out that this was the highest point in Wales and is commonly used for special forces training. After cresting the peak, we took a few pics with the National Trust rock (which indicated the service's commitment to maintaining the park) and headed back down.

Coming down the mountain was where we really felt the last four days of walking as the toes of our shoes bore the brunt of the g-force in trying to slow our descent. With each step, the toes would slide forward and bottom out. Ow, ow, ow, as we took each step down and forward and tried to maintain speed. Scattered sheep were watching, laughing, and wondering what the big deal was. We finally made it to the bottom and got offered beers by those who had stayed in dedication.

We fired up the bus and continued our journey north. Along the way, we stopped at a decent pub with a Chili's-like menu of meat pies and brown sauces and then continued the drive through the beautiful mountain towns of Western Wales on the way to Southport. We eventually rolled into the Vincent Hotel, which would be our final lodging hub to play our next four rounds. This marked the halfway point of the trip and anything resembling standard UK-like weather kept getting pushed back further in the forecast each day. We had been super fortunate to this point with all sun and no wind and were getting a little spoiled. Maybe we were just feeling guilty.

MTB: Why I did it; the fun.

OTB. Why I quit. Too many times.

Mom, too young to go.

My sister Kelly; wife Nicki; son Jason; me; daughter Taylor, Mom (Karen) and Dad   (Ron).

My dad and his Caddie Jimmy. Oh Jimmy!

My first caddie experience. Brian Horn, Tim Breland and me.

Bushwood! I'm home.

Tom Vaughn. Iron Man.

The ROTA: a trip of a lifetime.

Instant friends; just add beer.

The Penfold Hearts; paying (and playing) a tribute to 007.

Whiskey Gold as a prize.

Royal stockings. Hard to believe they could make my legs look skinnier, but they did.

The Royal St. George's Starter. The original grandfather clock.

Royal St. George's 4th hole.

Members only at RSG.

Barney checking out history.

Barney, JoeBro, Erik, and Dobler take a dip in the Channel

"Balls Deep" game. Anyone got change for Euros?

Wilk ordered three sticky toffee puddings and ate them all.

Roz in the Sarazen Bunker

The Brecons Beacons Hike

Lechyd-da! Heading into Wales

The Great House. "Cozy!"

! MIND YOUR HEAD !

Alan is big at the Great House.

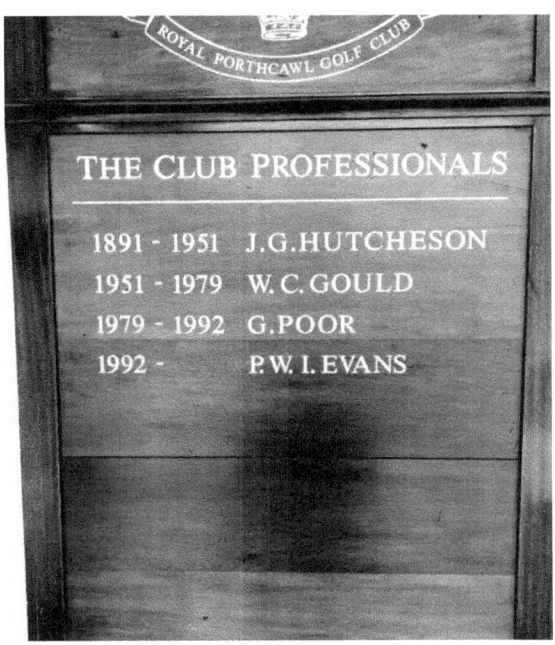

Not much turnover at the Porthcawl.

Big Alan Stearns swingin it at Formby!

Roz with a tough lie at Birkdale.

Gary and Harry tell tales of "Fooking" Ivan.

They love their pies. Meat or other.

1891-1892
W.W.P. SHATWELL

W.E.

I hope he knows Lord and Lady Douchebag of Sandwich.

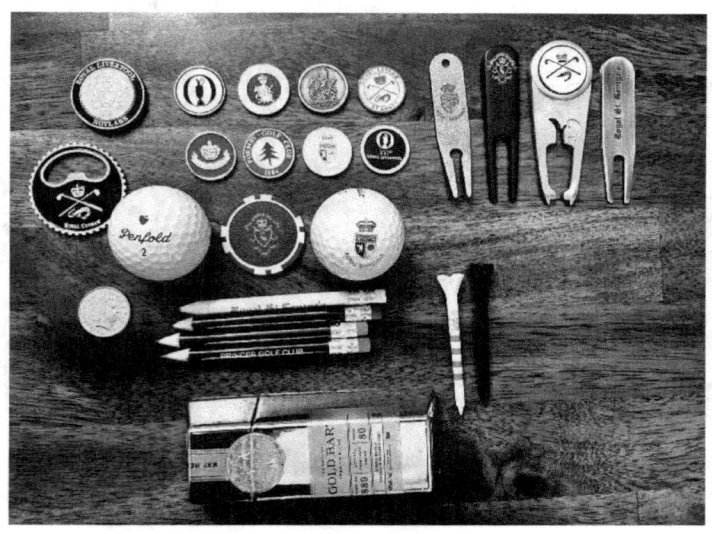

An accumulation of memories.

The Taps
Aug 16, 2022 · ⚙

A massive Thank You to our American golfing friends for visiting us these past few days.

The Taps
Pub

See menu

A salute to the yanks on Facebook.

Royal Birkdale. So unique

That thing was real!

Seniors in training.

An impossible stance. Max double.

JoeBro going for a sandy

Roz, Barney, Dobler, and Murph.

Getting cleaned up for Liverpool

Four babies' butts with smiles!

A narrow escape for me.

The practice green at Royal Liverpool

Sunset at the Prince's Lodge. What a venue.

Caddie Luke and I.

A final meal of proper Fish and Chips. Time to write a book.

The Rota crew. From the left: Chad Roesler, Brad Barnett, Erik Hansen, Alan Stearns, Scott Wilkinson, Conrad Roberts, Joe Brotherton, and Brian Murphy

Royal Lytham & St. Annes – Course 5, Day 6

Too much of a good thing...

The second half of the trip started out easily enough – with a light breakfast in the Vincent Hotel after a welcomed good night's sleep with the assistance of climate control. JoeBro and I ventured out toward the waterfront afterward in search of over-the-ankle white socks needed for our demanding Royal friends. While heading down the main promenade we looked right through a side street and saw, of all things, a Ferris wheel. Not sure what to make of it, we decided to go check it out. Upon further inspection of the area, we noticed a park with amusement rides and everything, a veritable promenade. Swan Pedal boats sat in wait for patrons on a beautiful little lake akin to Central Park. But I'm sure I have that backward as almost everything here is older than what we have in the States.

We continued on our sock mission and wandered in and out of the local groceries but had no success. It wasn't until JoeBro spied a local "BigMart" that was part bargain basement, half bomb shelter for discounted goods. There they were, Umbro soccer packs for 5 quid. Paydirt! We both grabbed a set for our partners in crime back at the hotel. JoeBro and I would take great pride in watching our fellow compatriots don these Umbro stockings during today's round. Mission accomplished.

The shuttle filled up early for Royal Lytham as Roz told us we were going into Lytham St. Annes to meet some of his old friends Gary and Harry at the Taps pub before the round. As it turns out Roz had stayed with Gary and his family while working out here years ago, so a reunion was in order. Honestly, I wondered about us getting soused before our round of eighteen at such a prestigious course with over one hundred and seventy bunkers. What would the Royals think? No matter, for we were men…and we hadn't quite visited a true pub, yet which was something I was really looking forward to.

The Taps pub had a long history of supporting the local links, the RAF (Royal Air Force), the local Rugby, and just about every other activity in Lytham that could be followed with imbibing on a pint (or ten). And boy, did it deliver. They even went as far as to install wall-to-wall, real grass turf during the Women's Open Championships in 2006.

The Taps was stationed just off the most beautiful town square I've ever seen, so I decided to take a quick lap around before joining the group inside. Alan and Wilk joined in and reminded me that it was time to start looking for something to bring home to our wives. I wandered down a few streets with shops and found nothing, then headed off to the waterfront where I found some amazing riverfront windmills and brick churches of unique value to photograph. With my wandering tourist soul quenched quickly, I returned to the Taps to find my companions having a pint and a bit of conversation with Roz's friend Gary and his friend Harry. While I played catch-up, Gary treated us to stories of the pub but most entertaining, were those of "Fooking Ivan from China." Granted, we need to take this with a grain of salt, because the initial meeting of Gary and Ivan was a long time ago. As the story goes, the initial interaction was simple enough, but the name has stuck for many a year. The simple question was "Hey, Ivan, what is your Chinese name?" Ivan simply replied; "It's *fooking* Ivan!!"

Gary continued with another story in which Ivan was clearly perturbed that the local RAF base would have helicopters circling the military golf course while he and the lads were playing. The nerve. As it turned out, Ivan had an ace up his sleeve being a graphic designer. So, he put together a fold-out sign to stow in his golf bag. One day, while he was trying to putt out, an RAF Blackhawk chopper was hovering incessantly overhead. Having had enough, Ivan reached into his bag and began to unfold his latest design to send a message. The message was not spelled out in text but instead in a picture... of a middle finger. We roared laughing. The joke was good, but there's something about the way the English tell jokes that make the good ones great; they just sound funnier.

It was still early at the Taps, so the staff was kind enough to let us take a group picture behind the bar before it filled up with patrons. It had already been a great day and as the bill landed on our table it was at this moment (if you've been paying attention) that "Operation Euro Wash" came full circle.

"Oh and hey...who the f%#*'s been passing out euros??" said the Mountain known as Wilk.

Uh oh.

I looked over to Wilk as he pulled out money to pay for lunch and I saw it. A euro ten-spot in his billfold.

"Where in the hell did these come from?"

I shrugged my shoulders and he continued, "We asked Neil to do us a favor the other day and grab some ciders while we were playing and I handed him like twenty euros!...he looked at me like I was an idiot...I don't even know where they came from?!!"

Alan was laughing with both his face and shoulders bouncing as he and Wilk looked in my direction. Being a stand-up guy, I made a mock look over my shoulder to see who I might blame for this crime...and there was no one. Just me.

Alan said, "Hansen might know."

I fessed up, but not without making it look like I did it deliberately... like some professional money- laundering operation with me at the wheel as the mastermind. We laughed our butts off and continued the ruse, making up stories and multiple scenarios that sounded even more ridiculous.

At this point in the trip I'd been to a few pubs, but The Taps was the one I had envisioned in my dreams. I hoped I could come back someday and bring an army of friends. It's that good.

Being done with our lunch, we hopped aboard our Scottishpiloted chariot and headed to the course. The ride was a quick ten minutes and led us to a small neighborhood area where it looked somewhat impossible to be home to an Open rotation, eighteen-hole links course. It was further inland than any links course we had played thus far. We really hadn't noticed the ocean as it was a few blocks from the beach but not obvious as part of the course in any way. I couldn't help but wonder, was it a true links course, not being close to the water?

Ironically, most people get confused in thinking that a links course is one that is simply flat with no trees, nor water hazards, but has large undulating greens and deep bunkers. However, the word "links" comes via the Scots language from the Old English word *hlinc,* meaning "rising ground, or ridge." True links land is typically characterized by dunes, an undulating surface, and a salty, sandy soil unsuitable for farming but which readily supports indigenous colorful fescue grasses. Together, the soil and grasses result in firm turf that allows for a different style of golf. The links-style course allows balls to "run" out much farther than on softer turf courses after a fairway landing. It does meet many of the qualifications although looking out from the parking lot, Royal Lytham appears to just be a flat course on a rectangular lot. I'd find out soon enough how naïve my thinking was.

***

Royal Lytham & St Annes Golf Club was founded in 1886 and the present course was constructed in 1897. The clubhouse celebrated its centenary in 1998. It is one of the premier links courses in the world, host to ten Open Championships, two

Ryder Cups, and numerous other major tournaments including the Women's and Seniors Open Championships.

It is renowned as a course on which it is hard to scramble a good score, after all, there are a hundred and sixty-seven bunkers peppering the fairways and surrounding the greens. It may not be the longest of courses, but it is one where careful thought and accurate shots are required.[7]

***

As we unloaded and staged for our round, I immediately noticed that the Clubhouse of Royal Lytham resembled a kind of doll house – perfectly painted and manicured with multiple shades of green, burgundy, and white trim. The grounds were also perfectly clipped with tall rectangular shrubs rising up from the soil and serving as borders for the property. It was almost dreamlike in nature compared to the other waterfront properties, which were more structured and weathered before they unleashed their golfing victims outward toward the open sea where the elements could eat them alive. I felt that its preserved state must be from the fact that it was so well sheltered from the surrounding neighborhood and therefore not exposed to the ocean-front squalls like Cinque Ports or Porthcawl.

As charming as it appeared, we were warned by Gary back at the Taps that Lytham and its bunkers could swallow us up quickly, so best to play smart and find purchase anywhere on flat land off the tee. Pocked like meteor strikes from above,

---

[7] "Royal Lytham & St Annes Golf Club." February 4, 2023. https://en.wikipedia.org/wiki/Royal_Lytham_%26_St_Annes_Golf_Club

these collectors of poorly thought-out tee shots would gladly gather in anything well struck or not and an attempt to escape in a forward manner would be forcibly denied. "Best to hit it out sideways." he told us, as the depths would have you facing a wall of shame more than once. So, the strategy for the day became simple: Do whatever it took to avoid those bunkers.

Being another one of the royal courses, it met my qualification for a full caddie to carry my bag while my mates chose a fore caddie to help search for balls and read lines. Say what you will, but after four rounds of walking followed by a hike (damn you, Dobler!), nothing sounds more like heaven than someone carrying your clubs like a links concierge. And though there was still the same disparity of four shots between me and the fellas, I was feeling saucy after those pints and hoping to gain some more ground in the games with the aid of a worthy looper.

Today, that looper would be Kevin. A retired policeman who found retirement boring, Kevin had a wife who was also "quite keen a player," as he put it, and they traveled and played a lot of golf together now that they were empty-nesters. We enjoyed talking and walking as we headed off the first tee and with my "2-iron off the tee" strategy, I managed to par the first two holes; however, I then max-doubled on three, when we lost my ball by misjudging the distance as I hit it left off the tee.

I'm fine with misread putts and bad clubbing, but to me the most important job of a caddie is to help you find the ball. He'd been looping for two years and had a decent knack for picking driving lines and reading putts even though he missed a few. That was expected. But losing that ball, which we all saw bounce a couple of times, was hard to live with. But it happens.

I quickly let it go, thinking I shouldn't have hit over there in the first place.

What was crazy about these links courses is that despite the greens being undulated, there wasn't much break. This made it all about speed, and it's hard for caddies to know the putting speed of their daily, one-time loops right out of the gate. Besides, somehow, with my right-brainedness, I make more breaking putts by leaning on my creative side; however, give me a straight putt, with little imagination, and I'll find a way to miss it... every time. And that I did.

Miraculously, on that day, Kevin and I were managing to steer clear of every fairway bunker on the course, which again, was my only real goal. I soon found out, though, that was not enough; in fact, approaches need to be steered perfectly to the green without so much as a frog hair of draw or fade unless planned. The greens were not small, but like most links' surfaces any stray shots to the elevated edges would bounce sideways or backward and be sucked like a black hole into the perfectly placed bowls of sand on the periphery.

My favorite example of this came while standing on a large fescued hillside hump after a pulled tee shot. Kevin the caddie warned me to, "Avoid that mother f&%#r (bunker)on the left of the green at all costs... Tiger was in there and took eight in the Open." That's all I needed to hear to permanently cement that swing thought and deliver my ball perfectly from wispy, mounded hump to the aforementioned hell...like a magnet. As my 6-iron swing came back down on-plane toward the ball, the rough grabbed the hosel, forcing the club head to turn over just enough to produce a nice little draw. I thought I hit it perfectly as I watched it carry the bunker and even bounce once or twice. But, like at Porthcawl, it didn't have the forward muster to get over the nose and rolled backward like a missed skee ball attempt – and down into that mother-f%#king bunker. I had to laugh.

Moments later, standing deep within and looking at the face of that thing, I was just hoping to get the ball out… which I did with a mighty swipe and the laid-open face of my sixty-degree wedge. But, like most of the shots out of these purgatorial pits, it allowed for no spin, meaning it hit the green and ran like a scalded dog off the back into the tall stuff. I managed to get it up and down for bogey from there with a really long putt, which made me feel like a hero, if only for a moment. I've come to find that there is such a thing as a great bogey… and this, was that.

As I said earlier, on a trip like this you really hope a caddie just adds to the experience. That means stories and all. Kevin shared some great stories about Bobby Jones and other greats winning there, but, most remarkably, on 18, he said, "Gents, I want you to think about something. Some of the best players in history have been in a position to win the Open Championship here at Lytham and as they walked up to this last hole, they all wish they could just make par." He continued, "So, you're in great company, let's see if you can too."

I started great, by hitting a really nice drive down the right side. "Adam Scott would have given anything to hit this drive where you hit it," Kevin said, "Instead he lost it all here hitting into the bunker on the left." Feeling proud and relieved (for a few minutes anyway), I blasted my approach deep left behind the green, and almost into the pro shop. All I wanted was par, but felt humbled and scrambled for a bogey – and a bad one. Oh well, the golf was still good, and this course had been great.

A bogey-bogey finish was not what I had in mind to end the round, but it was good enough for Roz and me to take the honors in the blind draw. I could hear my name being half-muttered and cursed out of the side of Alan's mouth ("Damn you, Hansen") as I canceled one or two of his skins with my strokes. Sorry, buddy. All totals in, he granted me another outright skin which added up to three or four to this point. I'm trying my best not to acknowledge my skins that came with a stroke, but it's how the handicap system works and I take comfort in the fact that I didn't invent it.

Hate the game, not the player.

As the round ended, I decided to head back to the gift shop and call Dad back in Arizona to see if he wanted anything. It was finally late enough there to call and confirm and catch up a little. We chatted about how he was enjoying the pictures of our trip online with his new companion, Beverly. It had been just over a year since Mom's passing, and he and I seemed to be recovering as well as anyone could, with great friends, relationships, and the great game of golf. All he wanted was a green Lytham golf hat and so I picked it up...no problem. But, as I came out of the pro shop, I saw Neil walking at me with a serious look on his face.

Problem?

Traveling is never easy, especially abroad. On this trip, every-one in our group was flying into London Heathrow and head-ing north, where they would depart for the States out of Man-chester. Easy... except for me. When I had booked my flights (or when my amazing wife booked them), we used rewards points, which was great, right? Well, this meant that I had to fly into, and out of, Heathrow. So, when Neil was to drop the boys at Manchester on Saturday, August 20, the plan was for me to hop the train down to Euston Station and visit some work buddies in London stay the night, then fly out the next day. No problem.

Problem.

Here's the thing, America. The Brits love their rail system. Highly efficient and effective, it's big money. They have us beaten there. It's also Big Union. The last time I was in Lon-don, there was a threatened strike. From my experience work-ing in big Telcom, strikes were a threat, but only once in a while did they *actually* strike. Not this week. This time the Brits were serious. Day after day, the threat of a strike when I was planning to travel loomed with the unpredictability of a rain cloud.

The daily news covered both union and railway representatives as they pitted their positions against each other. As a result, no tickets were available on my needed travel day of Saturday, Au-gust 20, and other options like car rentals and buses booked up quickly. I'd hoped that when I got to within a week of the trip the threat of a strike would clear. Nope. Instead, because I had waited, I was relegated to renting a tiny clown-sized car to get me from Manchester to London. It seemed to be my fate, and

I just accepted it as the trip progressed.

As I was coming out of the Lytham pro shop with my dad's green hat in hand, our driver, Neil, informed me that his next golf group coming to town was supposed to take the train north from London, but, due to the strike, now needed a ride from LHR up to Manchester. So, he'd be going down to LHR to pick them up after dropping our boys off in Manchester and could now give me a ride!!! Yes!!

When I heard this news of a free shuttle ride to my airport, I hugged Neil harder than I'd probably ever hugged anyone in my life. Poor Neil. I nearly picked him up. I hope he didn't mind. But the good vibes didn't stop there. Barney shouted out,

"E...We're going back to the Taps!!"

YES!!!

Now on cloud nine and with the rest of the crew excited for me, we headed back to The Taps for another pint (or four) and to meet back up with Gary and Larry, along with Gary's wife Beverly and their daughter Charlotte.

As we entered the pub, we were greeted with a homecoming of shouts and cheers by those we met earlier (and some of whom never left!). Throughout the evening Gary would introduce us to anyone he could grab, and he knew everyone in the bar. One such person was Mark, a big, bowl-hair-cutted fella looking like John Daly if he were a redhead.   He asked me, "What are you drinking, mate?"

"Old Speckled Hen."

He asked me if I knew the origin of the name. I replied that I did not.

"The Old Speckled Hen is not a chicken or rooster or even a bird…It's a car, mate!"

Perplexed, I said. "No way, that doesn't sound right."

"Yeah…it was a car manufactured by MG!" he replied.

"No way," I repeated, and challenged him with a look on my face.

So, we googled it together.

***

In 1979 the MG Car Company celebrated the fiftieth anniversary of its move from Edmund Road, Cowley, Oxford to Abingdon. They asked Morland & Co. to brew a special commemorative beer for the occasion, for which they would suggest the name. The "Old Speckled Hen" was named, not for a bird, but a car: a paint and rust-spattered MG Featherlight Saloon. Back in the day, this was the MG factory run-around, fondly referred to as the "Owld Speckl'd Un" due to its mottled appearance after several years parked under the paint shop.[8]

---

[8] "The Story Behind the Brew." December 9, 2015. The MG Car Club, Limited.

I love learning new things, especially when it's about beer! Incredibly, this was the same beer I drink at my home course in San Juan Capistrano, California. And I'd never seen it anywhere else before.

After a few pints of the Hen and some fun conversation, Gary invited us to a nice restaurant right next door called the "Lytham House." We continued to eat and drink from their excellent selection of cocktails, beer, wine, more beer, more wine...you get the picture. Dinner came on time and was fantastic, so now, properly stuffed and soused, we received word that our shuttle master Neil was waiting for us outside for the ride home. We extended hugs and handshakes to our hosts as if we'd known each other for years. Barney even hugged the waitress. With respect, of course.

After a final handshake with Gary, I departed the restaurant for the shuttle and came to find an interesting predicament. There was Barney, surrounded by eight soccer hooligans drunk off their arses, chanting him on to pound, of all things, a Corona? It took some effort, but we managed to separate Barney from the cheering and shouting and get him on the bus unscathed. Turned out the lads had been giving Neil a hard time prior to our arrival.

One of them had grabbed Neil's arm and said, "Wot ya gonna doo old man if I want ta get on tha boos???"

Luckily, the likes of Wilk and Alan, at a combined fourteen feet tall and six feet wide, came out of the bar and cast a shadow

https://www.mgcc.co.uk/articles/the-story-behind-the-brew/

from the streetlight that turned the aggressive mood around. Neil said the teens all carried knives like we carried handkerchiefs, so he was always wary (I hoped it was true, actually, since no one I know carries a handkerchief). Feeling lucky that it didn't escalate, we hopped aboard and headed back to the Vincent. Dobler recommended a nightcap there, but somehow, we all steered clear. A wise choice.

Formby –
Course 6, Day 7

Clear Skies and Foggy Golf

"BLOOOODY 'ELL!!"** as the English would say. Morning came way too early, and I was so hungover I could only melt down the hotel stairs with full help of the handrail, and find the restaurant where we'd been having breakfast. It was a ghost town at seven-fifty a.m. and the bus was coming at eight-forty-five for a ten o'clock tee time. My head continued to spin throughout my buffet of standard eggs, sausage, and potatoes. It felt like it was going to be a tough day at Formby.

***

Founded in 1884, Formby was redesigned by Willie Park Jr. in 1912. Over the years the course has undergone some changes, including some in 1922 by James Braid. The course has been the venue for a number of tournaments and competitions over the years, including the Curtis Cup in 2004 and The Amateur Championship in 1957, 1967, 1984, and 2009. It has also been used as a qualifying course for The Open Championship in 1924, 1971, and 1996. It hosted the Staysure PGA Seniors Championship in 2021 and 2022 as part of the European Senior Tour.[9]

***

It was only a short while to get to the course but with the way I was feeling, I was counting the mile markers, each and every one of them, no matter where they might be going. I hadn't gotten sick since college, but with the combination of this hangover, the English food, lack of sleep, and boat-like shuttle ride, I feared this might be the day.

Can't this thing go any faster??? Come on Neil, just get us there.

I breathed a sigh of relief as I saw a sign that read Formby Golf Club, but then felt a massive rush of confusion as we blew right by the turn-off. In a sweat, I googled Formby to double-check the course location and it turned out there were two of them. I asked Neil,

"Are you sure it's not the one we just passed???"

"Yup, I'm sure, I've been there before," he said.

"Okay, just making sure."

---

[9] "Formby Golf Club." February 4, 2023. In Wikipedia. https://en.wikipedia.org/wiki/Formby_Golf_Club

After another looong ten minutes, we finally started to head through a neighborhood, and I saw signs for the "other" Formby. We were close now and I breathed another sigh of relief, but were those train tracks coming up? As a bus/shuttle driver, Neil must stop before crossing regardless of train traffic, which he did; but, then, just as we crossed over them, we saw the signals go off and the guard rails lower behind us.

"Good that we made it, lads, or we would have sat there another ten minutes!" Neil said.

You would have sat there, Neil, but not me, those junipers just outside your air-actuated door were calling to me like a siren song of hangovers.

It was that close. But I made it.

Once we came to a full stop in the parking lot, I shoved Roz out of the way in haste and threw myself out of the bus to fresh air and non-moving land – a final relief. From there I decided to head to the pro shop where I would bumble through some major life decisions like, "Should I take a power pull cart or not? Which ball marker should I buy?" I went back and forth, holding up the line and annoying the hell out of the local help. Finally, I settled on the power trolley. *Problem solved,* I thought.

After trying to figure out the power part of the power trolley my small cup of patience had overflowed, so I went back into the pro shop to waste more of the help's time in switching to the more basic version. *Problem solved, again. Maybe.*

I loaded up my clubs onto the archaic analog version of a trolley which was most likely built in the '70s. My bag fell off three times while heading to the putting green. I fumbled and tried to gather myself without calling more attention.

Out of the corner of my half-open eyes, I saw a guy hovering over the putting green side to side on a machine at (what seemed like) sixty miles per hour. He might as well be riding a broom from my foggy perception, but Dobler says it is a green roller. I've never really seen one but have heard about greens being "cut and rolled." This was the roll part, I guess (or maybe it was doing both), but I still felt like I was hallucinating. It looked like the printhead on a classic dot matrix printer sweeping side to side as it did its thing.

I also saw sponsor billboards everywhere. Did we enter a tournament? Like a real tournament? Is this part of the trip experience? Is this really the right Formby? Questions upon questions. People saw me wobbling and pulling my squeaky trolley and probably wondered if there was a tournament for the mentally challenged going on and I, one of the benefactors. But no, they were actually primping and manicuring the grounds for the Senior PGA tourney coming to town next week. I got yelled at by my group to get the lead out and come over to the tee box so we could get going.

Today's group would be Roz, Alan, Barney, and me, followed by JoeBro, Murph, Wilk, and Dobler. Now to play golf...and simply stand over the ball and focus...

You got this Hansen....no problem...ehhhhh...annnnd...

The noted sports psychologist Bob Rotella says that a good golfer must pass through three mental stages as he progresses in the game of golf (if he wants to get any better): Unconsciously incompetent, consciously competent, and unconsciously competent. I swear I'm not making this up. Google it. I'll do you one better, Bob, I think I'm consciously unconscious yet competent on the first tee and hit it straight down the fairway. No idea how. Oblivious, I lowered my head and walked off the tee as my little trolley followed along.

Though foggy (not the weather, in my head), the course itself was an incredible change of pace…

Trees!

Besides the first few holes on the Prince's Himalayas nine, I had forgotten over the first four rounds what they looked like, but Formby brought it all into the window of a landscape, much like the Monterey Peninsula in California. Mixes of lush greens, tan fescues, large grassy mounds, sandy dunes, all framed by incredible pinewoods (thirty-five of which were knocked over in the last storm named "Arwen.") Even the weather was Northern California - like with cool breezes and white, marine layer clouds that would burn off later in the day.

The pinewoods were guiding us along, giving us a renewed sense of distance and perspective as we navigated around a few tricky sections. I had no caddie here, which was probably for the best since I would have most likely just embarrassed him. Luckily, as the mental fog lifted so did my confidence – at least a little. I hit a few good shots here and there, but the short game was still showing to be my Achilles heel. I made a bad double when I was unable to get out of the green side bunker on hole 2. But on the 3rd hole, Roz somehow found my unfindable ball buried in the fescue after a bladed 9 iron went screaming over the green. I hacked it out to ten feet and buried the putt for par, still a little unconscious.

The rest of the front nine went on with my partners playing pretty well and me just surviving. Still, I loved the course. I got two incredibly bad breaks which killed my skins effort on this outward leg, but I didn't mind, considering the circumstances. Today was all about survival and we were halfway home.

Having just three-putted, I walked off the 9th green and made the unconsciously conscious decision that the hair of the dog was the answer and bought a round of ciders for the fellas and me. I also opted to try something new – a pork pie – that was sitting on a baking tray behind the counter. Yeah, you heard that right. Pork. Pie.

I'd heard about the English infatuation with sausage rolls and pork pies from Tom's books. They are quite popular at the halfway houses on the UK links and managed to semi-nourish Tom throughout his travels with an unmatched sustenance-to-affordability ratio.

Looking like something that came out of an Easy-Bake Oven from Hasbro, this semi-small confection called the pork pie is, quite frankly, the definition of a gut bomb. Cleverly disguised as a baked sweet, its secret flaky crust hides a gruesome ball-shaped cut of pork-flavored substance within. Solid as a hockey puck and as cold as one on ice, this little number has probably wiped out more hangovers than Pepto. The body cannot possibly fathom the forces being thrown at it once the harmless-looking crust is crumbled, away exposing the mini ham-like brick inside. Upon consumption, I think all blood to the brain shuts off in support of building a front line for the tummy, Normandy style.

Dig in, fellas, there's a strong wave of ham hitting the beach at dawn.

Dobler explained that you could eat these warm or cold, but I had to ask, "Good God, man, can you digest it either way?" In hindsight, I did make a bomb for birdie on 10 after the meat pie so maybe Max Double should have one and leave me alone for a while.

Speaking of Max Double, he'd been hiding in the shadows for a few holes now on the back nine...lurking...maybe the pork pie worked. Oh, wait, there he is! Formby sixteen - an on-the-number, hundred-yard, par 3. We kind of laughed as we approached it. Come on! We hadn't had a par 3 under a hundred and fifty yards thus far and look at this thing...the flag was right there! We all swore we could reach out and touch it, yet after hitting the results were as follows: Erik - right bunker, Murph - in front of the left bunker, Roz- right bunker, Alan – forty yards deep. For my second shot, I had to come out sideways of my bunker and it headed over to the left bunker with a worse lie than the first! (see pics). Roz went deep, and Murph chipped it on.

Two Max Doubles and two bogeys, I think; it all happened so fast on this little hole it was like a punch to the balls by an

Oompa-Loompa. In fact, DJ, queue up a quirky Willy Wonka song about taking things for granted! Yes, shame on us. I also think the skins were washed at bogey among the eight of us! It's always the ones you least suspect. Well played, little No.16, well played.

We finished up coming in on eighteen and talked about how the pins have just been shoved out to the edges. We surmised that this must be to keep the other pin positions protected and unworn for the upcoming tournament. However, I will say this: I'd yet to see a bad green or even a ball mark. These links course greens are bomb-proof, so I don't know what the fuss was about. All I knew was that many pins had been ten paces off the high side, making it impossible to land and keep it close. Imagine a doorstop sitting sideways with a pin on the highest point and you're there. I short-sided at least five times on the way to bogey or, you guessed it, Max Double. But another eighty-four and one skin earned for the birdie on ten, all while holding down breakfast and a meat pie. Victory.

The group grabbed lunch and drinks in the clubhouse as we sat amongst the many framed pictures of past champions (most of them amateurs since they haven't hosted an open). As I walked out of the clubhouse, I saw a giant head of a hippo coming out of the wall at me. I shook my head, trying to make sense of it all. I think my head was still not right. Time to go.

Once back to the Vincent, I threw all my stuff to the sides and plopped straight down in the bed in hopes of falling asleep to Gogglebox on the telly. I was toast mentally and physically, so I decided to skip dinner with the group in favor of a light sushi menu in the hotel with JoeBro. I turned in after dinner and, as

I started to fall asleep, I couldn't help thinking of a saying my dad would use with regard to staying out late with the boys and playing golf early the next day:

"If you're going to hoot with the owls at night, you better be ready to soar with the eagles in the morning."

I was no eagle on that day at Formby; I was more like a wounded duck.

Royal Birkdale – Course 7, Day 8

Handicap Watch

"Games lubricate the body and mind."
– Benjamin Franklin.

I'll spare you the suspense: having gone to bed early…and not hooting with the owls again… was the right move.

Coming down the stretch with two courses to go and the money games still on the line, it was time to refocus and be competitive. At least that's what I like to tell myself. Honestly, as an amateur golfer, I just want to play, have fun, and hang out with friends. I don't have the competitive gene when it comes to golf as these guys do. Or at least I haven't engaged with it to the point where winning is more important than having fun. And I'm okay with that. Again, something I tell myself. I didn't know what Birkdale would have to offer us but from the history, it sounded like the Americans had done well there in the past. I also knew that it was one of the highest ranked courses in England and I was looking forward to playing it.

***

Founded a hundred and thirty-three years ago as Birkdale Golf Club in 1889, the club was awarded "Royal" status in 1951. Birkdale Golf Club moved to a new site in Birkdale Hills in 1894 and built a new distinctive art deco clubhouse in 1935. In early 1939, Birkdale was nominated as the venue for the 1940 Open Championship but the Second World War started in September 1939 and the Championship was canceled.

In 1946, the club finally hosted its first big championship in the Amateur Championship, won by Irishman Jimmy Bruen. During the immediate postwar era, the club also hosted the 1948 Curtis Cup and the 1951 Walker Cup, both won by the United States. With these successful stagings of important events, Royal Birkdale was felt to be ready for its first Open Championship in 1954 and has continued on the Open Rota ever since.[10]

***

We shuttled over to the course, which was the closest ride from the hotel thus far. Today it looked like Barney was the one who maybe had a few too many the previous night, or maybe just riding facing backward in the bus was making him carsick. Either way, no real issues during our short transport, but he too was ready to jump off the bus like I was the day before.

---

[10] "History." N.D. Royal Birkdale History. https://royalbirkdale.com/history/

As we came in down the main road, we saw the sign, turned off, and immediately noticed the clubhouse. Looking like a combination of a modern yacht and an old-time river steamboat, it was striking and non-traditional as a Royal. As mentioned, it was built in 1935 in the art deco style by local architect George E. Tonge when he won a competition to design the clubhouse. Tonge said, "I visualized the kind of clubhouse that I thought ought to intrude itself onto this lovely course. I imagined the lines of a liner at sea; the perfect balance of the ship at whatever angle and from whatever side it was seen." Not only was it unique, but probably a main topic of conversation for all who played here over the years.

If you remember the weather report from the beginning, we were looking at four days of heat and sun, then four days of cool and rain. None of the coolness had shown up and honestly, we were all looking forward to a little English weather as it had been sunny and warm every single day. The weather at Birkdale had turned…well, nasty. That is to say, it was cloudy and we might get a few drops of rain around one p.m. Ha! But would that justify the additional five pounds of rain gear in my luggage? Doubtful. Luckily, I had left the tags on, as it looked like the only rain we were going to find was behind us back at the top of the Brecon's Beacons hike a few days earlier. We should have enjoyed it then, and I suppose we probably would have if it hadn't been coming sideways at us riding a forty-mile-an-hour wind.

In front of Birkdale, we were greeted at the door with a smile and handshake by a representative of the club. He showed us around the lobby and gave directions to navigate the locker room and clubhouse. With the temps around sixty-three, we thought it best to put on long pants in the clubhouse and head to the first tee. We were introduced and greeted by the starter and my caddie for the day, John, both smiling ear to ear. The group was also introduced to our forecaddie, Steve.

John seemed close to my age with salty, grayish hair, and a decent tan for an Englishman. He almost looked Italian and could have pulled it off had he not had that fantastic and very typical English accent. He mentioned to me that his back was ailing him a bit, so he'd be carrying my bag on a trolley. Not a problem, I told him. As someone with a history of back problems, I could certainly empathize. We got to know each other a bit and settled into some golf talk while the others got ready to tee off.

Today's group would be Alan, Barney, Murph, and me. Unfortunately, Alan was already distracted by a nuisance client back home who he'd need to be on the phone with at some point later in the round. He was grinding his teeth, and I felt for him. There's nothing worse than having to work during a vacation, especially when it involves interrupting a royally expensive round of golf. You do what you can, of course, but these links courses demand focus and attention and without them, you might be in for a long day.

John and I settled on 3 wood to start, and I managed to hit another good first-hole tee shot which motivated us to a Par-par start. I was not sure how I'd been hitting such great tee shots on the first hole but clearly wished I could just play "eighteen first holes." It wasn't until I needed my short game on the third hole, a par 3, again, that it fell apart. Secret agent Max Double was back in my life for the moment, but I told him he could have this one if he left me alone today. I managed to hold it together and get through the front nine at forty-one or five over. With the lack of a short game, I'd take it. But honestly, that was another ho-hum nine and I hadn't shot in the thirties just yet, which surprised me. It was the middle of the rounds that had been unwinding on me so I decided to change things up a bit (like at Formby the day before) with a visit to the halfway house to see what they might recommend.

The gal stationed there was a pretty brunette with hair pulled back into a bun and dressed like a pro. Honestly, this was a fresh break from some of the other cranky and weathered old wankers we'd seen at the turn holding down the fort and selling ciders and meat pies with a salty disposition.

I noticed a bottle of a popular vodka on the top back shelf but with not much to mix it with, so she offered me some kind of sports drink. Just the kind of weird performance boost I need? Who knows! I nodded in compliance and bought yet another round of – you guessed it – Bulmer's Ciders for the fellas. I swear, those guys love their cider.

She gave me a double shot by "accident" with a "Whoops" and a giggle and asked how our round was going. I asked if they had anything to eat and the answer was a yes - but instead of a meat pie, they had sausage rolls instead. Sure, why not? I was thinking back to the results the meat pie came with yesterday. When the check came, I told her, "You know, you folks have been the most welcoming and professional of all the Royal Courses we've played and that's something you should be proud of."

She asked, "Which ones have you played?"

"Ha, all of them I think...let see..." I proceeded to list off our trip itinerary and she said, "Oh, wow, what a trip! Sounds amazing!"

After processing my transaction, I was sure to tip them via the machine (which goes to the whole course) and then gave her all the change I happened to have in my pocket. I had grabbed the lot of change on my bedstand before leaving the hotel and for those who don't know, the change stuff here can be one to two pounds each, and I had a bunch. I'm not trying to brag, I don't know how much it all was, but I happily gave it all to the team at Birkdale. Besides, I knew I could use a little karma on the inward nine.

Feeling good about myself, I hit a great shot off the tenth tee. "John," I said to my caddie, "it's a good day, man...with a funky drink in my right hand and a sausage in my left, we can't go wrong."

He looked at me.

"Wait, that didn't come out right...sorry!!! You know what I mean. Let's, er talk about the weather coming in...or the football...or anything else!"

We laughed it off, then made a good par on ten to get things rolling. Then we made birdie on eleven with a long snake of a putt no one thought was going in – including me.

Here's where I come to my favorite moment of the trip. The 12th hole is a two-hundred-twenty-two-yard par 3 that's into the wind, uphill, with a far-back pin placement. As if that wasn't enough, the green is surrounded by huge, tall-grassed mounds like a bowl so any miss left or right would summon Max Double for sure. I stepped up nice and relaxed with no expectation and launched a 2 iron that not only sounded great, but also looked great, flying pure and straight; never once leaving the flag. It had everything yet felt like nothing.

It was obvious that Murph's tempo had rubbed off on me just enough to get the club where it needed to be and not a millisecond too soon. We stood there and watched the ball carry into the wind without the normal ballooning or wavering off-track I was accustomed to. It was perfect in the moment. As good a shot as I've ever hit, and it looked like it had a chance to go in but landed just short. It would turn out to be about twenty-five feet short (dang depth perception). Who cares? It was a moment and one I'll never forget. As the Great Jack Nicklas has said, "A perfectly straight shot with a long club is a fluke.

When a player of Barney's caliber comes up and asks to see your club and says something to the effect of, "What the hell did you hit there…it sounded amazing," you take notice. You feel good. They hit these shots all the time. I don't.

Not more than a minute later, like an outfielder stealing a home run at the wall with an amazing catch, Alan got up and hit his patented trap draw with a four-hybrid and got it on just inside my twenty-five feet. Come on, man! He seemed to not care. I'd probably blocked him on too many skins with my handicap thus far so the gloves were off. But overall, two good shots and, if I can remember right, Barney and Murph had some short game work to get up and down for par. Nothing they couldn't handle.

My caddie John gave me the read and line for my putt. It was just outside left and uphill, so I hit it firmly and I buried it for my birdie. Next, it was Alan's turn. He missed his putt just outside the left. I actually felt bad. I was rooting for him, hoping he made it to lighten the mood and weight of his upcoming work call. You could tell the thought of it was affecting his round, when, a few holes earlier, he hit his ball down into some deep tall grass. As we all started to look for it, we heard, "GUYS! seriously…stop looking for my ball!!" He was over it. He took his Max and walked to the next tee box. We understood.

After we had all putted out and started walking off the green, out of nowhere, John came in tight with eyes wide and a huge grin face on the way to no. 13.

"Fooking two unda to staaat the back nyne ain't bad mate. Let's gooooo!!"

We were in this together, he and I, a team of misfits among pros trying to take it to the house.

Agent Max Double thought he would join in on the fun and spoil the party on 14th hole. I could hear my good friend Alan coaching my caddie way behind saying, "Look, don't worry about that; you just coach my guy in from here with pars on these upcoming par fives and he's got seventy-nine." That's how you know a true friend –always pulling for you even when he's not doing well, golf or otherwise.

John and I missed some reads for birdies coming in and I ended up carding a seventy-eight. My finest round of the trip, but it quickly gave me a hint of concern. With an eight-index coming into the week, cut down to a four, I'm still feeling a little guilty about blocking skins and/or winning them. No matter that I had carded an embarrassing blow-up round at Porthcawl (WITH Max double, mind you...it should have been much higher) eyebrows would be raised at this seventy-eight.

As we sat in the clubhouse telling stories of the round and adding up scores, I ended up winning a couple more skins on my two birdie holes. I cowered in my seat a little and tried not to celebrate. They were natural birdies won outright, but still, I'm notified by Barney that, at seventy-eight, "You're on handicap watch, EH!"

I had to tell them to check the handicap app online and they'd find nothing except sorry-as-heck scores sprinkled with a few moments of goodness, and that's all they would need to see. Having realized that's not what they wanted to hear, I mounted my defense with some sugar. "But what can I say, guys, a good course and good company brought out some good golf today." And now my conscience (either unconscious or incompetent), was clear.

Alan came in from outside having finished his call and joined us for a beer in the clubhouse where the blind draw was still being calculated. As luck would have it, who do you think got paired up in the blind draw? Alan and me. My seventy-eight and his eighty-sumthin. When blind partners were announced he shook his head thinking he dragged me down despite my good round. We won by six shots! Turns out we made a great team because we ended up having our good holes at different times making it a "ham-and-egg" moment and a perfect team pairing. Never give up. We finished our beers and hopped on the shuttle to head back to Southport.

A voice came from the back of the bus: "Hey, how about we go to one of those Turkish Barbers for a shave, fellas?"

In our short time together, it seemed only Barney could come up with something like this and he brought it up out of the blue. I was thinking, *I gotta vacation with this guy again!!*

All of us looked at each other and admitted we'd never gotten a real, full-service shave before. Heck, this might be quite cool. But then with my rising skins count, I was wondering if this wasn't a planned attempt on my life with a straight razor.

Regardless, when we got back Barney, Wilk, JoeBro, Murph, and I found the closest Turkish Barber Shop (which is a franchise over in the UK) and took turns getting cleaned up. This was really a great idea to get a full, hot towel service and come out looking and feeling soft as a baby's butt. Well done, Barney, and a fine idea to look our best tomorrow at Royal Liverpool!

For the evening dinner, the group decided on Thai food next to the hotel. After being seated, Alan began talking about all the courses we'd played. After all, tomorrow would be the crescendo. Which was our favorite? Will Liverpool live up to the hype? We tried to rank them in order, and some were calling Lytham their favorite thus far. Others preferred Birkdale (I know I did) and a couple liked St George best. Dobler is saying Liverpool might be a bit of a letdown with all the hype we'd been giving it, but then again, they are hosting the 151st Open Championship next year, so how could it not be great? When reading Tom Coyne's books, I found he had many ways of ranking them, such as "I'd fly back tomorrow to play this one," or "best of the Open Rotation courses."

What's interesting about these courses is that it's not about island greens or huge elevation drops, or even forced carries over cliffs. It's more about how well the designers used the land without having to move it. Subtlety is almost more important with the placement of bunkers, greens, and teeing areas while using the existing terrain naturally, without resulting to using a bulldozer. After all, machines like that didn't exist when these courses were built.

Alan, in an attempt to draw a relatable comparison, mentioned that ranking them may be like trying to decide which supermodel we'd want to date. It's a fair comparison, of course once we quickly got passed the preposterous notion that a supermodel would have anything to do with us. As we continued, we talked about how some can be beautiful and appealing on the surface but high-maintenance underneath. After eighteen dates, you may not like them very much.

With all the hidden hazards, grumpy bumps, humpty humps, and unseemly undulations we encountered, you may come out exhausted from any one of these courses and decide it's not your cup of tea. For instance, we loved Porthcawl for its incredible layout and beautiful clubhouse, but would I go back there to get kicked in the pills again? I didn't know. Part of me did want another shot at it but the other part thought that particular royal supermodel may be too high maintenance. We continued discussing well past dinner and headed back to the hotel. As for Liverpool, we would know the answer in less than twenty-four hours.

Royal Liverpool –
Course 8, Day 9

Don't Even Say It

We were keen to get another good night's sleep for the one-hour trip to Hoylake for our finale. Barney, Roz, and Dobler had stayed out a bit late and were a bit quiet heading to the course. Weather for the day was supposed to have recovered from its "lowly" sixty-four degrees and cloudy the day before in Birkdale. Back to sixty-eight, partly cloudy with a twelve-mile-per-hour wind. I was done asking myself if this was really the UK and had moved on to wondering what housing prices were in the South of Wales. With great weather and people as nice as this I felt like if I could afford it, I could live here and thoroughly enjoy it.

***

The Royal Liverpool Golf Club, is in Wirral in Merseyside, England. Also known as Hoylake, from the small town it resides in at the northwest corner of the Wirral Peninsula.

It was founded in 1869 on what was then the racecourse of the Liverpool Hunt Club. It received the "Royal" designation in 1871 due to the patronage of the Duke of Connaught of the day, one of Queen Victoria's younger sons, Robert Chambers and George Morris (younger brother of Old Tom Morris) were commissioned to lay out the original course, which was extended to 18 holes in 1871. Harry Colt, one of the world's leading golf course architects, redesigned the course early in the twentieth century, and it has since been tweaked periodically, mainly as a response to advances in equipment.[11]

***

We arrived at the property and, upon Neil's expert maneuvering through the narrow, brick-gated walls, found the ivy-covered, brick castle clubhouse bathed in morning gold. I hopped out and got no less than forty-or-so pictures from every angle. This was just in the nick of time as within minutes the clouds came in overhead and darkened everything, stealing away what could be a picture framed with gold leaf.

It looked like we'd be spending the day in and out of the sun, which was just fine with us. My spirits were further uplifted when we walked into the clubhouse to another fantastic greeting from the manager of golf.

Like at Birkdale, he explained our final process of preparation leading up to our tee times and walked us into the pro shop,

---

[11] "Royal Liverpool Golf Club." February 9, 2023. In Wikipedia. https://en.wikipedia.org/wiki/Royal_Liverpool_Golf_Club

where every type of golf gear donning the "151ˢᵗ Open Championship" logo meant we'd continue spending more than we planned to. I was texting friends back home with pictures of cool hats and shirts for me to pick up for them. I had asked most of my friends if they wanted something while I was out there, and most of them wanted a keepsake from Liverpool. Of course, it was two a.m. back home in California, and I figured that by the time I got back in after the round they would have chosen their prize.

We ventured out of the pro shop, having dropped a pretty penny or two, and headed to the range which sits on a wide, flat plot of territory between the first and fifteenth holes. It was unique in that that one had to cross the first tee traffic to get to, but at least it wasn't a mile away like some of the others. It also seemed to be a range where you'd get free balls but might have to pay for grass. There was simply none around.

Not feeling comfortable at all on my patch of dirt, I decided to start with the wedges as usual and work my way up through the bag to the driver. For whatever reason and, out of nowhere, I started to give the hosel a workout and shank my first few attempts. For those unfamiliar with the hosel, it's the part of the club that connects the head to the shaft. It's also (more importantly) not meant to make contact with the ball. If it does, it produces a shank. A shank in golf is a kind of mental castration. And, just like crashing a mountain bike, there are some fun nicknames for the shank too. "Hosel Rocket" is a good one. Being donned a "Shankapottamus" is also fun; but not today, not now.

I think there's nothing quite like being a Shankapottamus, hitting hosel rockets on the range of a Royal course. As I hit another one, I look around, half-expecting some kind of royal range official with slacks and a gold-logoed blazer to take note and approach me. I imagined him saying, "Sir, if you do not manage to find the clubface within the next swing, we shall have to ask you to depart the practice grounds posthaste!" Indeed.

I also conjured up the thought of an announcement coming over a pro shop loudspeaker asking me to start hitting the driver just to avoid the sound a shank makes. Believe me, none of these thoughts helped me find the clubface because golf is a mental game. In fact, my favorite saying about this situation is from Chi Chi Rodriguez and that is, "Golf is ninety percent mental, and the other ten percent…is mental." That's how bad it is.

I tried to adjust by standing a foot further away to avoid another hosel rocket but was now taking divots so huge I was afraid I might hit a sprinkler or sewer line. Had I lost the swing entirely since yesterday? Maybe. The boys were either not saying anything or just plain blocking it out. I dirtied up my nice golf towel by cleaning off my wedges, but with so much dirt I should have really used a pressure washer to finish off the job. With my head hung low, I meandered with my bag back to the clubhouse and practice green to help get my mind off what just happened. And it did, because the practice green was something I'd never seen before.

Immediately outside the pro shop, it was the length of the entire backside of the clubhouse and separated by an asphalt walkway. It was completely rectangular and about ten-by-fifty square yards with a giant mast from which to hang the international flags at the far end. It struck me as non-organic-looking, like it was built with a baking sheet.

After twenty minutes of practicing our speed and direction for this final round, we packed up and wandered over to our first tee, where I saw the two caddies for our group coming up. There was an older gentleman standing roughly five-seven and a young man of about the same height.

Come on, give me the wise, old green reading genius who's got a million stories, not the kid who's just getting started.

Contrary to my wishes, I was introduced to Luke, the "young'n" who would be my caddie. Darn. With a curly blond head of English hair with well-cut sides and steely-blue eyes, he looked like he was all of a royal thirteen years old. I was wondering if Mum didn't just drop him off for his loop. Turned out he was eighteen and, with his rosy cheeks and the look of an English boy band singer, I couldn't help but think I might stuff him in my bag for my same-aged daughter back home. It was about time she dated a kid who golfed. There goes my mind, over-processing things again.

"I could be this kid's father…wait… Luke…I'm your father…(in) law??" Heh! Let's see how we do.

In describing the golf course, Luke told me that the first hole was actually going to be the third in the open next year, which seemed strange as we're right in front of the clubhouse. He explained that in order to get the eighteenth to be a proper finishing hole, they'd use sixteen instead of eighteen, moving everything back a couple of holes. Fair enough. We all exchanged pleasantries with the starter, who handed our gift bags of logoed tees and markers, and we picked the final team order: Barney, Roz, Dobler, and me.

Let's finish this off in style, boys.

Hole No.1 (for us, at least) was a dogleg right, headed out toward the waterfront, dead into the wind and alongside the range to the right. The only thing keeping a ball from rolling into the range on a drive was a small, peaked mound about two feet tall, running down the border. If a drive had any sideways roll on it, it would be in said range and OB. It seemed almost unfair and weird at the same time, like a bowling alley with a reverse gutter. So much so, in fact, that I imagined myself hitting my ball into the right gutter only to have to turn and make that walk of shame back to my partners to grab another ball and try again.

Clear your head, man.

"Play left," Luke said, "Play way left." I did as he said and aimed left, pushing it dead straight down the middle — a good miss. We headed out and found my ball down at the bend of the dogleg, about twenty yards left of the OB mound which is right at the apex.

"Too close for me," I said to Luke, "But we got away with it."

Turns out Luke was a 6.5 index like I am now (Thank you, Birkdale), and had been a member of the club for the past five years. An eighteen-year-old member of five years at Royal Liverpool? Hoylake?

We lined up for our shot into the green. I'll be honest – at that moment, standing over my approach, I had a feeling that I've never had. I knew I was doing well on the skins and the blind draw games contending almost every round with my helping handicap. Even with my index cut in half, I felt so guilty about the winnings that now I didn't really care how I played. I figured I'd just play and enjoy the day and not worry about trying to win anything. And that's what I set out to do.

My approach into the green was on Luke's advised line and it missed left but was still on the short grass. I told him my short-game confidence was at about a two out of ten, so he handed me the putter. We two-putted for par and got on with it. Our whole group made fours. No damage done there. Most managed to par the next one too. Dobler birdied. We got to the par 5, third hole and the team managed two more birdies from Barney and Roz. They were playing well today.

Don't say it, Luke… Don't even say it.

We stepped up to the par three, or 4th hole, and it was into the fan (wind) about a hundred and eighty yards to a raised green with the normal, curse-word-provoking bunker to protect the short left. Dobler and I both hooked it left over the bunker, catching the green for the briefest of moments, only to watch it go down into a swale left of the green about pin high, but eighty feet away. Barney managed the front of the green and

Roz hit it in the bunker.

As we walked up and assessed my shot, I said, "Luke, hand me my 3 wood. I think I'll do the old bump and run."

Having given up on playing well and enjoying the day I found myself feeling saucy. I mean, why not try the stuff you see on TV in the major tournaments? And, I hadn't tried this shot yet on the trip, but it seemed prudent given the landscape.

With no bunker to deal with and short-mowed turf, I coached myself into a nice short swing with a heavy, slightly-lofted club. I essentially laid down a putted bunt into the face of the hill and hit it too hard, and watched it rocket past the hole. Luckily, it got held up by a backstop of fringe behind the flag. It funneled right to about twenty-five feet away. What came next was pure conflict. This had been my range all week: a twenty-five-foot putt, just outside the left of the hole. Knowing this, I didn't try to miss it, of course…that would be silly. But did I try to make it? I know it sounds the same, but it's not.

I made a good stroke. Uh oh. It went in.

Barney said, shaking his head, "That's just filthy, EH, just filthy!" He was right; I did feel a little dirty.

At this point, I was wondering if he could mean it. He's a great guy and I know he did, but to me, it's probably getting old to these guys. Maybe it was just me, but I felt it.

Luke said, "He's right…Bloody filthy par that was, brutha."

Again, feelin' dirty.

Okay, but don't say it, Luke, don't you dare say it!

We got up on the next hole and hit a good drive down the middle. As Luke and I walked down the fairway, he told me how he'd just finished his high school finals the night before.

"What's next for you?" I asked.

"Well, I'm heading to University in Bath to study sports science."

"No kidding," I replied, "I was a sports medicine major myself a long time ago."

He said he wanted to study that and sports psychology as well, so we talked about Bob Rotella and other great sports psychologists. It was great.

We arrived at my ball and the kid told me, "Man, I usually caddie for hackers, you guys are the best golfers I've ever caddied for. Is that group in front of you with you too? And you're way better than a six handicap!"

Damn you, Luke, you had to say it.

With that, I was feeling over-confident and probably headed over my skis as I considered next my shot.

Okay, Erik, you're playing pretty well, let's try a punch shot here into the wind 150, 7 iron...you know...like Rory McIlroy...or Tommy Fleetwood.

Sound the War Horn...Golf Gods Assemble!!!! With that last filthy par, those lofty compliments, and me thinking I'm someone I'm not, the golf gods reached down with a lightning bolt and connected my hosel with my ball sending it sideways into the fescue.

CLANK!

A royal shank.

Now, for those who've never shanked a ball during a round, it's quite, how do you say, "special." And by "special," I mean uniquely terrifying, affecting everyone who witnesses it. Like a fart in church, you can neither laugh, nor chastise, nor criticize; you can only sympathize. Granted, you can shake it off with a next, good shot if you've recovered mentally. But not me, not this time. Like most Shankapottamuses, you grab the club harder trying not to repeat it. This just makes it worse.

Next shot from the rough with a fine lie; CLANK, shank! Then my chip, shank! I swear I would have shanked my putt had my partners not picked up my ball for me. I just laughed in disbelief, but Luke didn't. With his head down, he did his best to acknowledge none of it. He was right to do so.

With that exhibition, I was put in my place for the rest of my round. But I just embraced it, relaxed and it helped me hit some better shots. Honestly, I kind of felt better knowing I was not winning anymore today. In fact, I felt great…even liberated. I know it sounds weird, and I don't mean to sound cocky, I just felt very guilty about winning anything as the new guy. So, I vowed not to try.

As a result of the attitude adjustment, the pork pie and pint at the turn (yes, I dared brave the pork pie frontier again) somehow tasted impossibly better and the sun came out to see us down the backstretch. We played some incredible holes coming in and hit shots into the wind that were dead on, only to roll off the green and be sucked into those darn bunkers again. The 15th was just such an example and worth a mention.

Not a long hole at only one hundred thirty-four yards from the tips, the 15th hole (meant to be the 17th at the '23 Open) is the newest of the course. Surrounded by natural, menacing dunes both fore and aft and pot bunkers to the sides, there is plenty to keep you busy if you miss the green. And this would be totally understandable given that it plays directly out toward Dees Estuary, causing most shots to balloon into a prevailing wind and end up in peril.

I don't think one of us was able to hold the green from our forward tees, and some tried twice! Having seen the results of this devilish design, I couldn't wait to watch the Open Championship as I was sure this hole would be a constant of entertainment.

On 17, we felt our round and trip coming to an end; but we were not done yet. There was still a test at hand. And that test was a dead-into-the-wind, four-hundred-yard dogleg right with the 16th hole to our left mirroring us but coming the opposite way. The number two handicap.

Roz hit a good one. Barney pulled his slightly left and Dobler hit a beauty. With the day I'd had after the fifth, it wasn't going to be a great round, but as I was looking at the scorecard, yep, it was a stroke hole for me.

Maybe a last chance for glory?

I let my excitement get the best of me and thought of hitting something tricky and fun. So, with the driver, I put my ball mid-stance and teed it low, hoping to catch it on the downswing producing a low trap-draw (like my good friend Alan). Sounds like a solid plan into the wind, right? I took the club back and brought it down for contact. The rest went like this:

"Tower to golf ball, Tower to golf ball, we're going to go ahead and redirect your target approach dead left to fairway 16 on heading Whiskey Tango Foxtrot...repeat new heading on WTF. Please acknowledge."

New heading acknowledged Tower, proceeding dead left to fairway 16.

The result of my poor execution was a sweeping dead hook left that found the *middle* of the adjacent sixteen fairway.

"Aw, Erik, that's so bad!!" I chastised myself outloud. Or... ?

Luke said, "Nooo, ya coot like fifty yards off the hole, man.

Nicely dooone…you're goonna to have a straight shoot in frooom there noow!"

I laughed.

So, you're telling me there's a chance, yet again.

We approached the ball with haste as we noticed the sixteen-tee box starting to fill up with golfers who will want to *selfishly* hit to their own fairway.

Luke said, "One-ninety into a dead wind…better to play it two-twenty…"

He had proven himself to be a good caddie thus far and without request, instinctively handed me my 2 iron. I stepped up quickly so we could get this over and get the hell out of there. I took the club back…you can imagine what happened next…

No shank. Instead, I crushed it!

It made the same noise as that pin-guided missile I hit on the 12th at Birkdale. Only it was low. It was beautiful. I looked at Luke and, like Shooter McGavin (*Happy Gilmore*), threw my club to him for stowage and said, "Is that any good, buddy?…Now let's get out of here!" We then began to evacuate the area immediately.

Golf gods, are you still up there? Why, yes we are…what did you have in mind?

Now, in a slight jog, I looked back to the ball still in mid-air and began to notice something…something right in front of the green – a small hump. I guess I didn't notice it in our rush, or I didn't care. Doesn't matter. Like a tiny round sentry guarding the hole, this hump deflected the ball two feet left of center and sent it into a pot bunker. I just know Max had something to do with this. It was a bad break, but I was okay with it. Luke and I hoped it was a good lie and that the ball rolled down into the middle, so I'd have room to get it out. With some skill and some luck, we hoped for a sandy par and a net birdie.

As I prepared to step into the bunker, we heard "FOOOOORRRRREEEE!!!!!" coming from the sixteen-tee box. Somehow, Luke ducked instinctively just as the ball flew right over his head. Without that call of "Fore," and no perfectly-timed duck, Luke might not be with us. It was that close. All I could think was,

Who the hell would hit it that far left??!! That's a dead pull hook! I mean…oh right, me…ten minutes ago…forget I said anything, people!

Now rattled and unfocused, I bladed my bunker shot thin over the green, and with my mouth wide open into the wind, got a pie-hole full of sand…probably more than was under my ball. Damn you, Max Double!!! One more hole to go.

Our final hole, no. 18 is downwind, so it should be easy. Dobler hit an absolute bomb at about three-hundred and fifty yards and chipped up links style for an easy birdie. A thing of beauty. The others made par and I missed my usual five-footer for par to close it out with a bogey.

Really? A double bogey, bogey finish? Ok, let's try to turn a positive into a negative…well, I guess at least I didn't play well enough to win anything. I just may be invited back after all!

Golf done!

It was bittersweet. Bogey or not, it was still a beautiful round at Royal Liverpool, and I couldn't wait to watch it on TV for the Open Championship. We snapped some pics and I managed to get a quick, personalized tour of the private clubhouse sans golf shoes and hat to round out the experience. We hopped on the shuttle and headed back to The Vincent for the day.

We decided on Chinese again for our final meal. The final rounds also needed to be added up. No cash has been paid out thus far, so it all comes down to this. Of course, I hoped to do well in the standings overall but not at the expense of moans and groans at the new guy taking it all with his fat handicap. Thankfully my bad round today would set the tables straight. We settled down to the same table we ate the first night we were in town and the waitstaff remembered us right away. Drinks and apps were ordered and while waiting on their delivery, we started reviewing the round and summing up the totals.

I was not really paying attention as Murph added up the scores with Barney hole by hole, but then I heard, "Okay, third hole, I've got four with a stroke…"

Uh oh…

"That's Erik."

Wait what? $h!t.

"Let's see… fourth hole…I've got a natural three here…anything better?"

That filthy par putt…no way…

"Nope," Barney said… "I got Hansen here…. with that filthy putt!!"

Whoops…

I slumped down in my seat. Then it went Dobler with one, JoeBro with one, Roz with one, and Barney (from a killer chip in birdie), and then Dobler again for two.

Thank God that's over.

They went on to announce the totals over the trip and I ended up in first place for the skins. I pictured the ghost inside me slipping out of my body, thanking everybody like a Casper-like George Castanza and saying, "Thanks very much everybody…you've been great!" and drifting out of the room.

I'm probably not getting invited back. I can tell you one thing: if I'm anywhere near an eight handicap, I surely won't. Hell, *I* wouldn't invite me.

With a super-early pick-up for the airport Saturday morning, we turned in early to get packed up and get to bed so we didn't oversleep. We were golfed out…but would we play tomorrow? Probably.

The Final Transfer – Day 10

A Quest for a Pub

When Murph and Wilk came down the next morning, they notified us that their connecting flights out of Manchester had been canceled. Over the next two hours, Wilk tried to get customer service as our shuttle traversed the Manchester/Liverpool countryside (and coincidentally went in and out of cell coverage). When we arrived at Manchester airport and dropped off the rest of the crew, Wilk and Murph decided they had a better chance to get a flight out of Heathrow, so they stayed on board and rode with me and Neil as their efforts continued. As Neil was doing us all a solid, I tried my best to make the miles go faster and asked about his family's travels in the United States as well as other topics. I felt he appreciated that, and I simply enjoyed getting to know him a little better.

After dropping Murph and Wilk at their terminal, Neil dropped me off at my hotel just outside of Heathrow with a hug and a goodbye. I headed through a revolving door and up to the check-in desk. The clerk was a young lad around twenty-three years old.

"Mr. Hansen, sir," he said, "we're unable to check you into your room just yet; however, I can check your bags now and there's a lovely pub just down the street." He saw my golf bag and asked,

"Did you play some golf?"

"More than I've ever played," I replied.

He continued, "I went to an indoor driving range last night with my mates and hit my drive two hundred and forty yards! First time ever trying! It was awesome...I think I'll start playing golf!" His infectious enthusiasm was far above the others at the desk, and it probably annoyed them at times; but was hard not to love.

"Good for you, man!" I replied.

It was then I remembered that I had a couple of ROTA hats left over in my suitcase, so I reached in, pulled one out, and handed it over to him as a gift for the kind recommendation.

I told him we'd played all the courses listed on the hat – and laughed, drank, ate – for nine days straight. I had also made six new friends, and it was all based on the greatest game on Earth.

"Oh, thank you, Mr. Hansen, sir!! Thank you!"

Ironically, while looking for the pub, I felt lost and doubled back, having looked around in disbelief as I found myself in what looked like a tidy little neighborhood. It can't be down here, can it? As I walked, I noticed an empty, poorly attended, grassy lot to my right with wrought iron fencing. The only occupants were two small horses who moseyed over to say hello and get a pet. I couldn't help but feel I was on the right path now.

Within a hundred yards, I came to a place big enough to be a house but hardly an inn – and yet it was. The Pheasant Inn was just the right amount of "cozy." As I took in the aromas of aged cedar, meat pies, and lagers, I noticed they had absurdly giant, bearded bartenders that barely fit behind the taps. To add more irony, the bar had many amusing "Watch your step" and "Mind your Head" signs, sometimes in the same spot. Yes, this felt like the right place to be.

The hostess sat me at a small table for two next to a window and took my order of a pilsner. While taking my hat off and putting it on the table out of respect, I looked outside, wondering if the clouds would bring rain. Minutes later, as the bartender brought over a tall pour of their local lager, the clouds parted, and the sun came through the glass to highlight the Rota patch on my hat and the golden pint right next to it. I took my laptop out of my bag and fired it up.

This looks like a great place to start writing a book...

A book about a golf trip.

Match Play

I felt renewed. It was good to be back home, and I was feeling like my old self again. It had been about a year since the bike crash and almost everything was healed and working normally, except for one small thing: the numbness in my left digits. While the doctor was still more than happy to operate, he mentioned that if it was not keeping me from the things I like to do it was best not to go under the knife. I'd made the decision to part ways with my love of mountain biking and reunite with an old flame: golf. And, with grip of a club, tying of a shoe, or many other mundane tasks, the lack of feeling in my left index finger and thumb reminded me why. My riding friends kept asking when I was getting back out on the trail, and I simply had no answer.

The best news was that my dad was doing great and had reunited with a long-lost friend. (Actually, they dated back in high school!) She had lost her husband months before my mom passed, and to the same disease: Alzheimer's. And get this: they have the same last name – Hansen! The cosmos felt almost maxed out on this one, and it had been a wonderful development.

Before I left for England, I had been playing in a team match play event called the 4-Ball Championship. It's a two-man tournament and another member, Justin Hales, and I qualified by taking third in a tournament called the Monster. It was our first time playing together and he and I hit it off immediately.

Our golf games complimented one another. He was a "plus-one" (a plus handicap player was usually shooting under par in the high sixties) and could make birdies in handfuls with chip-ins and long putts at just the right moments. I was what he called a "deadly" eight handicap who could make pars when needed to keep us in the match and maybe a birdie here and there as a bonus. The partnership was a solid ham-and-egg agenda that was netting results. We had beaten some pretty good teams on our way up the bracket and had made it to the finals to match up against the men's club president Walter and his partner Austin. But then I left for England.

My eight straight rounds over the pond, along with witnessing such great talent, had driven my handicap down at least three shots, which was a big deal. It sounds weird to say that's a bad thing, but welcome to the world of golf and the handicap system where, depending on the timing, high scores are good and low scores…well, you get the picture. To compound our co-nundrum, Justin had texted me a picture of a scorecard while I was in Liverpool indicating that he had shot a course record sixty-two (a *net* sixty-three with a plus-one handicap!) at his home course, in of all things, a 4-club tournament. Yes, you heard that right – he only used four clubs! This meant we'd have to play better than ever when I got home.

Justin was an absolute assassin when it came to competitive golf and his aggressive play with birdies and eagles ripped out the hearts of his opponents, creating havoc within the team. I felt our duo had a great chance to win the final, but I wasn't prepared for the tectonic shift that was about to occur and how it would test my newfound intestinal fortitude.

Match day at six a.m., I get a text from Justin saying, "I'm so hungover!" along with a picture of him in the McDonald's drive-thru getting some junk food to process the bottle of wine he'd stayed up to drink with his wife.

Oh boy.

This witty, fun-loving ace of a golfer had spent the previous day playing and drinking with our buddies and followed it up with a bender back at the house. As a result, when he showed up at the course, his head must have felt like a fifty-pound watermelon because his eyes looked like pressured, squinty radishes leaking water. Our team just might be in trouble.

Okay, Hansen, it looks like you might have to take the wheel on this one and hold these guys off until he gets back on track.

Justin had more than done his part to this point and I needed – no, I wanted – to prove to myself that I could play under pressure…and succeed. And so, we set off.

First hole. After managing to somehow get his ball off the first tee, over the water and down the right, Justin bladed his second shot over the green and out of bounds. It had begun. He was already "in his pocket" (meaning he'd picked his ball up and discontinued playing the hole since his teammate -me - was in good shape). Luckily, I had hit a good drive and followed it with a nice wedge to three feet and made birdie. This would tie our opponent's birdie and avoid being down one hole with seventeen to play.

However, that would be the only highlight for us as the rest of the front nine went a bit rough – with me playing lackluster golf and Justin hitting balls all over the earth while trying to get some "hair of the dog" down and get back into the zone. He made a couple of pars but no birdies; however, his sense of fun and humor never left, which kept my head in the game for the most part. Seven straight bogeys in a row resulted in us being three down going to the ninth hole.

A long par three with water right and OB left, I managed to hit a 6 iron just onto the putting surface about thirty-five feet away to the right. Then it happened; I made a crazy-lucky putt that bounced and broke right-to-left and slithered in the bottom side of the hole. Yes! Now we're only two-down going to the back nine.

Even with a birdie, I, somehow, was not happy. A forty-one front nine was not what I'd planned, and I was shaking my head as I added up my score. However, in match play, it's best to forget the score and play it hole by hole, so my thinking about it negatively showed how few matches I'd played.

I had to shake it off and remain positive. I know that had I been in this position a year ago, I would have been upset and continued to force the issue. Now, I found myself being patient and letting things come to me without frustration. Yes, I think

I'm playing sideways, mentally.

Out of nowhere, Justin grabbed my shoulders with buddy-like force and said, "Man if you were to tell me I was only two down going to the back nine, I'd take it every time…I love the back nine! Let's go!"

Justin grabbed a Sea Breeze at the 19th hole (the clubhouse) in his continued effort to right the ship, and find the birdie god, as we teed off on ten. I found it best to stay away from any drinking and remain focused. He continued to struggle on the first two holes, but I was making pars now instead of bogeys, which was good. Then, on twelve, the Justin I knew showed up and made two incredible shots to the par 5, then a bomb-of-a-putt for an eagle to win the hole. I followed suit with a thirty-footer for birdie on thirteen to pile on the momentum. As we walked up to the next tee box, there it was: a row of fireball shots lined up on the curb of the cart path.

What the -? Who the -? Oh, hell no…

At this point, I was trying to figure out why the group in front of us would be buying us shots during a Championship match. Then a couple of things dawned on me. First, the group in front of us were buddies and board members with Walter, so either they were just being nice to us OR at some point a text went out alluding to my partner's lack of sobriety and that one more shot would put him over the top. And it did. If those shots were donated with dubious intent, I say bravo; it was a cunning move that could work.

After being peer-pressured into a fireball shot with the group,

I vowed to keep the momentum (while Justin continued to enjoy the wind-in-the-face from the cart ride like a golden retriever). I made one more birdie on 14, followed by a good par on 15. This put us two holes up with three to play. We had this one in the bag.

Or so we thought.

Our opponents weren't rookies, and they weren't just going to go away easily. They deserved to be there just like we did. And, at this point, that Fireball shot had more than succeeded, because while I was putting out on fifteen Justin was already on the phone with his wife to come to pick him up…while he sat in our opponents' cart! Laughing, I pulled him out with a big, "COME ON BUDDY WE GOT THIS!!" I urged him to buck up with something great just once more so we could pull this one out. Turns out 16 and 17 were *not it* as Walter and Austin hung in there to win both with a quirky par followed by a great birdie. So yes, like any great showdown, we now found ourselves teeing off on 18, back to where we started:

All square.

Standing on the tee box, I was feeling the pressure to come up with something great to beat our opponents as my teammate wandered around waiting to hit but completely checked out.

"You okay, man?" I asked, "You gonna make it?"

"Yeah yeah, I'll be mrmeremmmfmafmpfh." He trailed off with a wave of the hand.

Great. Looks like I'm on my own. Let's not end it with a loss. Focus!

A short par 3, all four of us managed to hit it on the green with myself being closest around twenty feet to the right, and Justin being the furthest at forty feet, and just on the front of the green. Walter and Austin were about the same distance at about twenty-five feet, but one was above the hole and the other was below. I was sure that they were probably thinking the same thing and that was: no one's going to make their putt…and we're going to playoff holes.

Hardly able to stand and seemingly out of the picture, Justin lined up his putt…and gave it a firm stroke…

We watched maintain its speed and line, thinking it was a great lag-putt to get it close…

As it approached the hole, it bounced a couple of times and lost some speed, but was holding on…

"Oh my god!" I shouted as we watched it crawl over the front of the hole.

Remember, my fourth version of Bob Rotella's unconsciously competent, unconsciously unconscious?? This…was that! I almost came out of my shoes and cheered him and gave him a big hug. I felt so bad at my outburst and apologized profusely to both of them. Our opponents were understandably beside themselves at what just happened. Both missed their putts, solidifying our win and my first championship of any kind in golf. With four birdies on the back and no bogeys, I ended up shooting forty-one, thirty-one for my best round of the year with a seventy-two.

As I finished adding up the scores and began to unload my stuff from the cart, I noticed Justin's bag was already gone. Thinking he'd loaded his car and was going to come back and celebrate until his wife arrived, I didn't pay much notice. However, Justin never came back into the clubhouse. He just went home.

I'll be damned … a walk-off win. How fabulous.

The 19th Hole
(Epilogue)

I was walking up the largest hill of Newport Beach's 15th hole, my feet already sopping wet as I followed in the muddy footsteps of my predecessors. I was trying to embrace my second go as a caddie here at the 2023 Hoag Pro-Am, however, I was finding it hard to find much joy right here, right now.

If you remember, last year's experience of caddying at the Hoag involved a ton of legwork in preparation for what turned out to be a cakewalk. Well, things had made a major about-face that year as, with a golf bag over each shoulder, we start the first hole of two eighteen-hole rounds. If you're wondering if you read that right, I'll reiterate:

Thirty-six holes…carrying two golf bags.

In my head, I was remembering that comment from Caddiemaster Joe last year; that they've only had to physically carry clubs…like once in the past ten to twenty years…because of the rain.. Somewhere in Scotland, there's a barrel-chested caddie laughing at me.

I was thinking it's Jimmy.

I had been looking forward to this week for three hundred and sixty-five days straight – ever since my first caddie venture at Hoag had me riding in a golf cart like a royal liege serving my kings as they walked with the pros. I had shot yardages and raked traps with loads of time to spare and even chatted with the other caddies up on the tee boxes and greens with plenty of breath left in our chests. But not this year; this year had become a mess.

In the weeks leading up to the Hoag Pro-Am, Southern California was having its wettest winter in thirty years. It was as if Nature was trying to catch up from year-over-year drought situations in one season, and the now-favorite phrase "Atmospheric River" was being thrown about by the media like the days of the East Coast's "Polar Vortex" every time you watched the news. The forecast, which had shown a major storm hitting the day before the Pro-Am event, had been the object of our unwavering focus for the past week and a half. No matter how much I cursed at my phone's weather app and no matter how many other apps I loaded, it showed this monster storm system bearing down right on time and ruining the plans of a lot of people.

As we got into the three-day window, the text we had all feared came from caddiemaster, Joe:

"Hello, Gentlemen,

Well, the rain is coming and already the Tournament decided no carts will be allowed and every caddie will carry both bags in your twosome on WEDNESDAY.

If the course can't handle the rain, we'll double bag again on THURSDAY.

If anyone has a problem with this, I need to know right away, please!"

Wow. Just like that, the pillowy caddie experience we'd had a year ago had been turned upside down by the removal of a simple piece of golf equipment-the motorized golf cart (Yes, the very same Florida-made invention I lamented earlier in the book.)

Not only that, but I had also been looking forward to another (more well-planned) visit from my friend Tim Breland as I would caddie for him on Wednesday, followed by his boss and my main man from last year, Chris Cairns, on Thursday.

The storm came in as forecasted Tuesday evening and dumped a record three inches of rain in a single night. How lovely.

The thought of carrying two bags in the rain was something we had laughed about under our breath and all the caddies admittedly feared, but the thought of doing it two days in a row scared the hell out of everyone. Although the text had gone silent upon the possibility of a painful experience leading to no-shows, when the time came, the caddies showed in force to support Joe and Lesley, who, everyone knew, were up to their ears in scheduling mayhem. I'm not sure if you heard, but putting on a golf tournament is a mess at best, and throwing a little monkey wrench into the mix like torrential rain and cancellations would result in pandemonium.

Looking down the barrel of double bags for thirty-six holes for two days straight, I pulled my sixteen-year-old son, Jason, out of school for backup. I had no idea how many holes my fifty-two-year-old body (with two back surgeries) would hold up for, and my offspring could be my savior. However, the more I thought about it, the more I liked the idea of sharing this experience with him and teaching him a trade that seemed to be making a comeback at local country clubs. The thought of missing school (he's a straight-A student, people - don't worry) to make an average of one-fifty per loop had Jason dreaming of parts purchases for this new mountain bike. If you're thinking the apple doesn't fall too far from the tree, you're way off; in our case, it's clearly a nut…from a nutty tree. In any event, he too was excited at the proposition to make some extra dough.

As we arrived at the course on Wednesday for the first round, there was a slight glint of hope as the golfers and caddies showed up; but when the rain started coming again the golf course called the whole day of play *off* - for only the second time in three decades.

The call to cancel was disappointing but certainly understandable—especially when we saw the damage we were doing to the turf the next day, with only one tee shot under our belts.

For the Thursday round, my co-caddie was Corey Shumate, who I'd met at the Farmer's PGA Pro-Am in January. That day, which entailed a single eighteen-hole carry loop at hilly Torrey Pines, had us walking and talking with pros Colin Morikawa and Kevin Streelman while we looped for Farmers Insurance reps. It was an awesome experience and Corey and I had become fast friends, which was why I invited him to join me here for what was supposed to be a cakewalk. Welcome to the $hitshow, buddy.

Corey, though just forty years young, is somehow retired from a well-managed career in finance and wants to become a full-time caddy. So, he dismissed my apologies for the situation and told me he needed the work. Still, I couldn't help thinking he was cursing my name under his breath as he traversed this soggy hill with his own two bags, looking uncomfortable as can be.

As the Thursday Pro-Am started, we were to be paired with Mike Weir, the Masters-winning lefty from last year. I was looking forward to hanging with Mike again, but as he walked gingerly up to our group, he explained that he had hurt his back the night before and would be unable to play. The players liked Mike a lot and were a little let down when we got the news, but some things work out even in bad situations. Up walked Paul Stankowski.

Paul had been a journeyman over his career, which is to say he'd been on a few tours, notching seven victories across the PGA, Japan, and Korn Ferry. Paul introduced himself by jokingly stating the obvious: that he was "Not Mike Weir"; "not left-handed," and had "one less green Jacket than Mike did" – all with a deadpan delivery. We laughed. Oh yeah, and he wanted to have some fun. With that, we saddled up on our cart and, by way of the perimeter of the course paths (to avoid driving on the course) headed out to our first shotgun hole, no. 15.

Within the first few holes it was apparent that Paul didn't just want to be a pro who played alongside our players; no, he became a brilliant host and then some. Throughout the round, he not only chatted up the group but also took video of the amateurs' swings, gave instruction, and even adjusted my player's driver in hopes of a better result off the tee. In the end, he had taken our lemons… and made lemonade.

We finished up the round at an incredible four and a half hours, and the long cart ride (back around the perimeter of the course) gave us about seven minutes to rest, grab lunch, take some Advil, and hop on another cart; and do it all over again.

Corey and I looked at each other and you could tell we were dreading the thought of another eighteen with two bags. NBCC wasn't the hilliest of courses but it wasn't flat either. It would be a rough go, but we were committed and, like so many others, wouldn't let our caddiemaster down.

The second round had me back in front of Chris Cairns, my favorite loop from last year with a new partner, Dave Rousek. A third member would also join to walk along: Dave's boss, Gregg Reber. Chris was great to reunite with and had recovered from his near-broken toe from last year. True to character, he had also read the communications from the caddie tent asking all players to swap out any large, heavy, cart bags, and any other ballast in favor of lightweight stand bags – and he complied (as did Dave, thank God).

Brian Horn also came out to see us off and, upon watching us shed unnecessary weight, offered to stow Chris' regular shoes in his locker for the duration of our round. Once again, I found myself surrounded by good, thoughtful people.

Our pro for this second round was Jose Maria Olazabal, another Masters champ (two times, to be exact) from Spain who had a fantastic career with thirty professional wins on the European and PGA Tours. He was also a stone-cold assassin in Ryder Cup events, racking up points with Seve Ballesteros and

Sergio Garcia as they dominated the United States over the past twenty to thirty years. With a bit of a language barrier, he wasn't as chatty as Paul, but there was an aura of greatness to him no doubt. He helped with a number of putts with the amateurs, but his input was limited as he struggled to find his own game throughout the day. For me it was a pleasure just to meet a Spaniard of such great talent.

As for Chris and Dave, they were great to caddie for; in fact, Dave even offered a little assistance. As we turned for our back nine the sun came out (signaling some hope to this death march), but by that time I was mentally and physically done. Dave and Greg must have seen the look on my face, along with my slowed pace, as the lactic acid continued to buildup in my legs. As a result, Dave offered to carry his own bag for a bit. Then Greg jumped in and insisted that he carry Dave's bag. After one hole, I started feeling guilty and offered to help carry one of Corey's bags! In the end, the rotation of bags and ballast got us to the finish line with a smile and a great story to tell. But we were still exhausted. We all shook hands and were glad to be done.

I just hope I never have to caddie like that again.

Feeling forty pounds lighter, Corey and I almost skipped down to the caddie shack to get paid out. Joe handed us our payment envelopes and reached out and to shake my hand, but noticed me shaking my head in disbelief. He said, "Thank you for hanging with us on this one; you in for next year?"

And without hesitation, I replied,

"Wouldn't miss it!"

251

In Closing

Looking back at the progression of this last year (while writing the book), I relish the perspective it's given me. I've learned that taking a pause to think, recalculate my aim and direction, and make a proper decision, has played the biggest part in my recovery. In fact, I've come to recognize that as negative as 2021/2022 were, I now see them as a gift of learning more about myself and how best I deal with things. Now, when life starts fighting me, I do my best to just step aside while it keeps on swinging, and maybe even punches itself out to reveal a weakened state with which I can cope. With confidence I can say I've used this strategy successfully, and on multiple occasions; however, until this point, it's been only in small fashion.

As I write these final paragraphs and try best to convey these new angles on life, I find the words to be blanketed in irony. I speak of my current career situation. While I'm thankful it's been a worthwhile endeavor, like many of you, I find I'm playing in the proverbial rough way too often. On top of that, I feel there are simply no fairways left to recover to - and that's no good. In conclusion, I've decided I'm taking everything I've learned, everything I've experienced, and putting it to work – by leaving my work – and somehow, somewhere, find another course, another fairway.

I'm actually excited.

I'm playing sideways.

Course Rankings by My Overall Experience

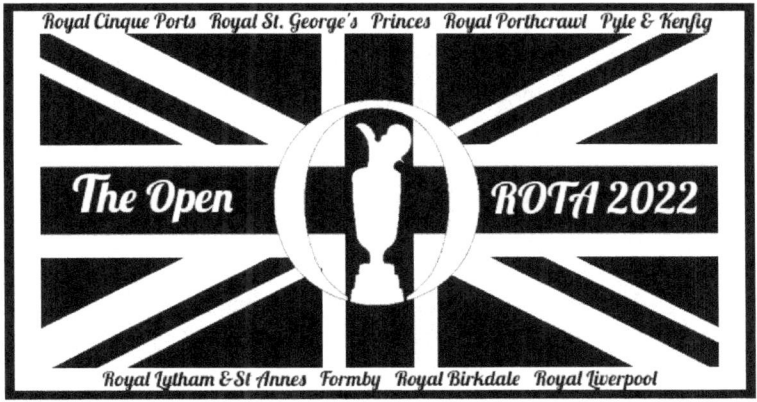

Royal Cinque Ports Royal St. George's Princes Royal Porthcrawl Pyle & Kenfig

The Open ROTA 2022

Royal Lytham & St Annes Formby Royal Birkdale Royal Liverpool

I feel it's important to note that these are placed in order based on my experience only. These rankings are not a reflection of these courses at their best or worst since I've only played them once (and not even that well). These are just the comments of a traveling amateur golfer. I would play each of these courses over and over if given the chance and there were parts I loved about each one of them, with their variations in character.

1. **Royal Birkdale** – Okay, I probably shouldn't have to start this way, but hear me out! Yes, I shot my best round there, but that's not why I chose it. The course was challenging but not overbearing in design. No two holes were the same which offered tons of variation.

The clubhouse was gorgeous, and though wildly untraditional it had the perfect mix of accommodation and luxury with an incredible view of the 18th hole. The kids (man, I sound old) in the pro shop were super nice and attentive and the shop had a great selection. The practice areas were the best of the bunch. The staff and facilities were above the rest, leading to a perfect experience for me overall. In the end, we were treated more like royalty here than anywhere, and this was a royal golf trip. Had it not been the "worst" weather (cloudy and sixty-five degrees) of the trip I think my fellow golfers might agree.

2. **Royal Lytham**- This was tops on most of the guys' lists and probably the purest links experience. With a perfectly manicured clubhouse and practice area hiding a visually deceptive viper pit out in the wind, the Lytham layout looks fun, flat, and easy until you tee off; and experience over one hundred hidden bunkers lying in wait. The clubhouse was small and beautiful, with loads of history. A pint in the clubhouse may have taken it to the top for me had we enjoyed it a little more, but the Taps pub was calling for us back in Lytham.

3. **Royal Porthcawl** - This course's location, layout, and spectacular ocean views put it high on the list. As dry as a bone, it still offered a complete test of golf requiring many unique shots. The clubhouse is small and quaint and does not stand out in its architecture, but the view is incredible. The staff was great, and the practice area was okay. We loved meeting and hanging with

a few members after our round as well. Mr. Lewis Mainwaring was a highlight and fine representative, but it's a shame his name won't be there on the Pro's plaque as he heads off to dental school. It's also clear from the plaque on the wall in the pro shop (pictured), which lists only three head pros since opening in 1891, that no living man has ever given up the position, making it near impossible. If I had one course to replay, it would be this one. It kicked me in my dimpled balls too many times during our short round and I want another shot at it.

4. **Royal St. Georges** - An incredible layout with shot requirements well beyond my abilities. It was probably an off day but had the pro shop staff been a little more welcoming and the clubhouse open to guests it would have ranked higher. I can't even imagine playing the back tees or in the wind (or both), but the course was understandably a little beat up and dry given the lack of rain. Still, I can imagine it in good shape and with the combination of James Bond folklore and blind quirky tee shots and approaches I'd play it again as much as I could.

5. **Royal Liverpool** - Hard to believe this one landed so far down but the competition is fierce. The course was interesting with some great holes, but there were several that were just plain simple with little imagination. The finishing holes of 18 or even 16 (for the Open next year) would both be downwind and easy, and the driving range location and condition were not up to par so it felt like a bit of a letdown. Still, Hoylake had an

amazing clubhouse and unique putting green which I loved. The staff was very nice, and the pro shop was, well, very expensive (for me, at least). I will play that 15th hole over a million times in my head (hitting the green once or twice) as one my favorite par threes of all time.

6. **Princes** – The Course - With a more modern club-house and three nines, this was unique for a true links, but I liked it. The Himalayas nine seemed to be liked by all for its variation and tree-lined fairways at the start. The spot where Captain Lucas landed his Spitfire and the Sarazen bunker made for good nostalgic spots to stop and read about the history, making us feel special to be there. The Shores nine was also beautiful as it ran along the ocean, but it felt a little basic. Still, it was in better shape than most and I enjoyed it very much. The facilities were good, with a great range and gigantic putting green that is joined to the 9th hole on the Himalayas! I've never even seen that.

The Lodge – An amazing place in and of itself, this is what really sets The Princes apart from the rest. I highly recommend staying there, regardless of the courses you play. Although its proximity to any of the local course clubhouses (including Princes) is a drive not a walk, the combination of a hotel, pub, beachfront access, and a fantastic putting green for fun and games, make it a wonderful overall experience.

7. **Formby** – I was very impressed with this course, due to the combination of a unique non-royal-designated

name and my lack of familiarity with it. The three holes going out were just okay, but then the fun started. Lots of elevation kicked in with some interesting holes that funneled us out toward the coast and back. The fact that they were having a Senior PGA there the following week meant it was in great shape, so that definitely helped. However, the final holes coming in lacked imagination and soured the finish for me. The clubhouse was nice, and I annoyed the staff to the point where I was apologizing for my hungover behavior. My bad, Formby. My bad.

8. **Royal Cinque Ports** - This one was the perfect one to start our trip and, to be fair, I may have missed a lot here because we were rushed getting on and off the course. It had a great proximity to the ocean but with a large dune-like wall blocking the view, you didn't see it much being recessed down behind it. It must be a major test of golf in the wind, but on this day it neither wowed nor felt boring. It was just good. The clubhouse and pro shop were a bit dated (no pun intended, since they were built in 1892) but it's possible that in our late arrival, we didn't get that chance to really enjoy it. Many consider Cinque Ports to be one of the finest courses in England.

The End

About the Author

Erik Hansen is one of those guys who doesn't know what to do so he tries to do it all – and sometimes even succeeds! Bottom line: he loves new challenges. A lifelong lover of sports, he studied sports medicine at Long Beach State University, where he also helped coach D1 Women's tennis while teaching kids on the side. However, his career path shifted dramatically to video after he spent seventeen weeks documenting the famous marine life artist Wyland as he painted walls along the East Coast. Erik's work has become more technical over the years, though his creative side continues to push him to design and build anything he can get his hands on. Currently, he works for NBC/Comcast as a Sales Engineer, designing those binge-worthy streaming experiences you find yourself addicted to. He has also returned to golf as his primary sport, and recently won his first team championship at his home club of San Juan Hills.

From building race cars in his garage or on TV (and even dumping one into Long Beach Harbor for the "Red Bull Flugtag"), his experiences in life, love, and loss have led him to start writing for the first time.

Raised in Northern California, Erik now resides in Southern California with his wife Nicki and their wonderful daughter and son, Taylor and Jason.

NOW

GO

PLAY

GOLF